SAVE YOUR MARRIAGE

How To Rebuild Broken Trust And
Reconnect With Your Spouse No
Matter How Far Apart You've
Drifted

SHIRLEY COLE

Copyright 2019 © Shirley Cole

Legal & Disclaimer

The following document is reproduced below with the goal of providing information that is as accurate and reliable as possible.

This declaration is deemed fair and valid by both the American Bar Association and the Committee of Publishers Association and is legally binding throughout the United States.

Furthermore, the transmission, duplication or reproduction of any of the following work including specific information will be considered an illegal act irrespective of if it is done electronically or in print. This extends to creating a secondary or tertiary copy of the work or a recorded copy and is only allowed with an express written consent from the Publisher. All additional right reserved.

The information in the following pages is broadly considered to be a truthful and accurate account of facts, and as such any inattention, use or misuse of the information in question by the reader will render any resulting actions solely under their purview. There are no scenarios in which the publisher or the original author of this work can be in any fashion deemed liable for any hardship or damages that may befall them after undertaking information described herein.

Additionally, the information in the following pages is intended only for informational purposes and should thus be thought of as universal. As befitting its nature, it is presented without assurance regarding its prolonged validity or interim quality. Trademarks that are mentioned are done without written consent and can in no way be considered an endorsement from the trademark holder.

Table of Contents

Introduction

Having to navigate the murky, confusing world of relationships is one of the trickier aspects of being human. Any relationship can be difficult, but romantic relationships are the most confusing and hardest to handle of all. When it comes to romantic relationships, it doesn't get much harder than marriage. When you swear vows to another person that are meant to last until death or divorce, you enter into a formal bond with that person. Regardless of the relationship you had before or the time you've already spent together, getting married changes things significantly. Ending a marriage is not a relatively simple task like breaking up with someone, but a complicated and lengthy legal procedure. When you get married, the whole nature and atmosphere of the relationship you have with your partner changes. Suddenly, things are far more committed and serious, even though nothing physical has changed. You both still look the same, sound the same, even feel the same as you did when you were dating or engaged. What has changed is your attitude and mindset, along with that of your spouse. It's a subtle change, one that you might not even notice at first, but it's there. You're both in it for the long haul now, is the thinking: for better or worse.

When you get married, you undertake a different stage in the journey you're on with your partner. There is far more expectation placed upon the relationship by both you and your friends and family. People talk about you differently and make references to the fact that you're now married. Again, the effect is subtle and the change often unnoticeable. After all, you might tell yourself, you're still the same couple you've always been. If anything, you can only be more in love now, right? Things can only get better from here because you're legally bound to one another. While marriage is certainly a beautiful and fulfilling experience, it can and does add a certain extra level of strain to things. Particularly as after you get married, you're statistically more likely to consider buying a house, have children, and look for more challenge and financial reward from your job. The strain created by being married and all the life development that comes with it can put you under an immense amount of pressure. It also has a nasty habit of bringing to light other difficulties in your relationship and personal lives as a result. This is why the divorce rate approaches fifty percent of all marriages. Making a marriage go the distance is a very hard thing to do.

In the not so distant past, divorce was not a common occurrence like it is today. In fact, it was very difficult to get a divorce at all unless you had a satisfactory reason. The culture of the time was that once a couple married, they stuck together through thick and thin. Of course, this didn't mean that people simply forced themselves to be happy — miserable married couples have always been a common occurrence — but they found a way to make it work. These days, the comparative ease of getting a divorce has seen divorce rates skyrocket. People are often quick to blame their spouses for the problems in their life and relationship, and can easily convince themselves that the grass could be greener with someone else. Often, though, people who remarry are even more likely to divorce again. At some point, you have to stop blaming your partner, look in the mirror, and take full stock of the reasons why your marriage isn't working. The alternative to doing this is a lifetime of failed relationships and miserable marriages.

If your marriage is broken and doesn't make either you or your spouse happy, it's a one-way road. Sooner or later, you're headed for divorce. The problems you face won't just go away of their own accord. Working through such issues is a matter of being able to change the way you view them in the first place. Throughout my career as a professional therapist, I've seen the same problems over and over again. When I meet the vast majority of my married, counseling-seeking clients for the first time, fixing the issues in their relationship and saving their marriage is their main priority, but it's something that feels perpetually out of reach. There's always another argument, another flashpoint for conflict and another fight. Sometimes there's been lying and infidelity, so perhaps the trust they shared is gone. Their marriage is on the rocks, and they're looking for a way to save it. My role is to step in and try to alter the way they view their marriage, their problems, and themselves.

It's not enough to just help a couple stay together, however. There's no point in convincing someone not to get divorced if they're going to live a life of misery instead. There are a lot of married couples out there who do just that; they stay together, miserable, rather than seeking happiness apart. Not only does their marriage need to be saved in such cases, but it needs to be overhauled and changed. The love and passion need to return. If a couple's sex life is AWOL, it needs to be found. In order to save your marriage, you need to not only stay together but be happy together. You need to be fulfilled, you need to want to be together, and you need to break new ground and rediscover the intimacy in your relationship. Through the techniques in this book, all that is possible. Not every marriage can be saved, but all that is required to save any marriage is the willingness to do what is required to make things work. That's it. That's all it comes down to. If both parties are willing to put forth the effort, there is no obstacle too tall for you to climb. There's no mountain you can't summit together.

Throughout my career as a professional therapist, I've built up a great deal of experience in making things work between married couples. I've seen it all. There is nothing that can shock me. I've seen closets with more skeletons than clothes and much, much more. One thing I've learned from all of this experience is that there's no such thing as a marriage without hope of getting better. Sure, sometimes there are two people with no desire to make it work — but in these cases, there's nothing left to save. When neither person wants to take the action required to fix things, there's nothing to be done. When it comes to the circumstances themselves, however, there is no set of events too difficult or too tough to move past when both people are willing to do what is necessary to make things work. I've coached couples who thought their relationship was far beyond repair return to being happy, mutually appreciating, and loving partners. I've seen spouses with the worst track records imaginable go on to be fulfilled and satisfied with their marriage. If they can make it work, you can too.

Saving your marriage is about embracing a new lease of life. You enter into a new stage in your relationship with your spouse, where you let the past be the past and focus on living well in the present and creating a better future. With this book, you'll be able to leave the petty bickering, arguments, and bad feelings behind and instead enter a new way of being together. It will help you focus on the joy in your life, rather than the misery. It will allow you to look at things more positively and show you that attitude is everything when it comes to making a marriage go the distance. It represents the culmination of my fifteen years of experience as a professional family therapist and is the sum total of the advice and expertise I offer to my clients. Over the course of my career, I've successfully coached hundreds of married couples on how to save, improve, and overhaul their marriage to stop the rot of a miserable coexistence and embrace the beauty of sharing a long, happy, intimate bond with each other that lasts them the rest of their lives.

This book contains the information you need to save your marriage. It will teach you the attitude and mindset that you need to cultivate to make things work with your spouse and change your marriage for the better. If you want to turn things around and embrace a better, happier marriage and a more fulfilling life, then read this book and get started on your journey to peace and joy. I promise you that if saving your marriage is what you want to do, then this book will equip you with the tools you need to not only rescue your marriage and uphold your vows, but to reinvent the nature of your relationship with your spouse completely. So, what are you waiting for? There's no point in spending any more time living a life that isn't satisfying or fulfilling. Break the cycle of misery now and by reading this book and finding out how to save your marriage!

Chapter One:
Improving Communication

We all know how to communicate. It's one of the most fundamental components of being human. We don't all know how to communicate well, however. There's no place where good, positive communication is more essential than in a relationship. It can make all the difference when it comes to cultivating a positive, joyful, loving marriage. In this chapter, I'll be taking you through why great communication is so vital and how to implement it in your relationship with your spouse to make a real difference.

The Importance of Good Communication

Communication is about a message being transferred between two individuals, a sender and a receiver, or speaker and listener. We encode information via language and transmit it to be decoded by someone else in order for them to decipher our meaning. Through this process, we can deliver insight into the internal worlds we experience and work to better understand one another, as well as deepening our knowledge of ourselves; speaking is a part of thought, and we have to talk to understand how we truly think about something. This is why we all have internal monologues of thought where we 'speak' to ourselves with words.

Communication is a skill. When we're good at practicing it, we're more effective at the whole process of sending and receiving messages. The more skilled we are in communication, the better we're able to explain what we mean and understand what other people are trying to tell us. Although most of us probably like to consider ourselves good communicators, the truth is that communication is relatively simple to do but very difficult to do well. The result is that most of the communication that takes place in our relationships and everyday life is incredibly inefficient. Both physical and mental noise along with other distractions can make the listener's job very hard and stop them from focusing on or otherwise listening to the words being said, resulting in a lot of meaning being simply lost in translation.

When it comes to marriage, being able to communicate well is vitally important. Any long-term romantic relationship represents an immense amount of time spent together and a very close level of interaction — in a marriage, this is amplified tenfold. Spending such a great deal of time with another person in overwhelmingly close proximity with so much at stake always leads to conflict and problems. When we spend enough time with anyone, we inevitably come to be annoyed by aspects of their being. The same is even true for becoming annoyed with yourself after spending too much time alone. Even couples that are very much alike will have vast differences in areas of their personality and preferences, leading to a range of issues from mildly irritating all the way to argument-causing, divorce-heralding ones. It's no wonder there's so much conflict in marriages. They're perfect, fertile breeding grounds for it.

The thing is, every person and every marriage has problems. In fact, roughly 70% of all conflict-causing problems in marriages are seen as unresolvable by both spouses; interestingly, this applies to marriages that are healthy, happy, and mutually fulfilling, as well as those that are burning down and heading for divorce. This shows us that conflict, problems, and issues in relationships are simply part of being human, and a marriage is no exception to this. There will always be issues and opportunities for conflict.

No one is perfect. What's really important, then, is the attitude that we take about these problems. A good marriage, a bad marriage, it doesn't matter — both have problems. It's the mindset and approach that we take to these problems that determine how good our relationship is, not the circumstances that cause the problems themselves. Having a happy marriage is about doing more of what works, and less of what doesn't — and good communication works better than anything else. Great, positive communication can make all the difference in your marriage, allowing you to work through issues that might otherwise derail things.

Differences in Communication

Everybody communicates in their own specific way, because everyone is individual and unique. However, there are also differing trends we can identify between the way in which men and women communicate.

Biological Differences

While there are always exceptions, evolutionary biology has resulted in men and women having certain common traits that are shared throughout wide swathes of the population that cause us to perceive communication and process meaning differently.

Men tend to see communication as serving one of two main purposes: either to make a statement or to ask a question. With men, everything tends to come back to problem-solving. They're wired to want to fix things, which is why they can often make such frustrating listeners for their female spouses, who get annoyed by them jumping in every time they think they have the slightest chance of solving a problem. Women, on the other hand, see communication not only as a means to an end but an end in and of itself. They often talk simply to express themselves, to work out how they feel and what they think, and to get things off of their chests. A lot of the time, women don't need any problems to be solved; in all likelihood, they already know exactly what they're going to do. They just want their spouses to validate how they feel.

Men, however, are far less likely to feel like they have to express themselves and be open about what goes on in their hearts and minds. They also tend to be conditioned by their culture and upbringing into believing that it's emasculating to express their feelings or talk about how they feel. A lot of men still buy into the idea that men shouldn't cry or show any form of weakness, and instead simply bottle up how they feel rather than getting it off of their chests.

Love Languages

Another difference in communication that's worth mentioning here is love languages. In a 1992 book called The Five Love Languages: How to Express Heartfelt Commitment to Your Mate, author Gary Chapman proposed that different people mainly express their love in one of five different ways. This can lead to confusion and hurt when half of a couple expresses their feelings of affection and love differently than the other. For example, one person might use words of affirmation in order to express their love, whereas the other may instead rely on physical touch to convey the way they feel to their partner. The end result is that neither person feels fully loved or fulfilled because they're both sending the right signals in completely different ways. The messages end up going over each other's heads because they're expecting to receive love in the same way that they express it.

There are widely thought to be five different love languages, as initially proposed by Chapman and verified by millions of couples ever since:

1. **Words of affirmation:** These are the spoken words we use to declare our love for our partners, such as telling them how much they mean to us, how much we love them, and how grateful we are to have them in our lives.

2. **Physical touch:** This refers to any physical or intimate contact we have with our spouse, like holding their hand, cuddling, and kissing them on the cheek.

3. **Quality time:** This is the time we take out of our lives to dedicate to being with our partner, enjoying their company and getting to know them better.

4. **Gift giving:** This is the giving of presents and gifts, and can mean anything from small symbols of love like making coffee or breakfast to paying for vacations and jewelry.

It's about the little thoughtful things we do for each other.

5. **Acts of service:** This refers to those things we do for our partners to show them we love them and that we care by standing by them and helping them out. It can mean things as little as giving them a ride somewhere or larger things like helping them out when they're in a tight spot financially or assisting them with a project they're working on just because we can and we want to.

If you can work out what your own primary love language is, as well as that of your spouse, you may well be able to better communicate your love and affection to one another by doing more to express your feelings in your partner's love language. You can also learn to better understand your partner's expressions of love by becoming more aware of when they're trying to show you they love you.

How To Communicate Well

When we're involved in the process of communicating with someone, we have one of two roles: we're either speaking or listening.

Speaking

Good communication is about understanding each of these roles and being able to practice them well regardless of the situation you're in or which one you need to use. When you're speaking, you need to keep in mind that you are first expressing to be understood. That is your main goal and priority — it should, therefore, be your primary concern, rather than speaking to persuade or to influence or inform. All of that is secondary. Speaking to be understood means focusing on getting an accurate representation of the message you want to send that is held in your mind across to the listener in such a way as to minimize miscommunication and misunderstanding. Your objective is to send 'A' and have the listener receive 'A' rather than 'B'.

When we communicate, we encode a message or meaning, in a language to transmit it to a receiver who then decodes the message to understand the meaning for themselves. The language we use influences how well this message is transmitted to our audience. Being an effective communicator when it comes to speaking is about choosing our language in a way that makes it easy to understand for our audience: the listener, whoever that is at the time. For example, if you were speaking to a child, you'd use simpler, less complicated language than if you were talking to a fellow professional in your line of work, in which case you'd use more specialized language to better make your point.

When you're talking to your spouse, you should try to express yourself as well as you can in order to make them understand where you're coming from. This is important in everyday situations like going to the grocery store or picking the kids up from school, but it's especially important when it comes to having difficult conversations where emotions are surfacing and you have to be vulnerable. Marriage is as intimate a relationship as it gets, and each of you needs to be able to open up to each other completely to make things work. If you feel like you can't be totally open and honest about the way you feel, then say so. At least be honest about that. Through simple heartfelt discussion and speaking the truth, a lot of progress can be made. Many married couples that have issues they feel just can't be resolved — when the fact of the matter is that they don't open up to each other honestly enough to even begin to resolve them in the first place. Marriage is hard, and talking about how you feel and why you feel the way you do is hard, too, but it has to happen. You should feel like you can talk about absolutely anything with your spouse, and they with you.

Listening

For most people, speaking is the easier half of the communication process. By its very nature, speaking is an active process. When we're talking, we're doing something proactive and creative. We work out what points we want to express in our minds and then put them into words in an ongoing process. Sentences flow together to convey meaning to our audience. Most of us can quite easily get into the zone when talking. It's only when we're distracted or run out of things to say or the right words to say something, that talking becomes more difficult.

When it comes to listening, however, things can be much more challenging.

Listening is a more passive process, as we're not constructing or encoding meaning but rather decoding it. While we still have to actively listen, we can easily switch off or become distracted without it being clear that we've done so. It's far more challenging to listen effectively because we have to pay complete attention to what is being said. We can't properly listen to what someone is saying and do anything else at the same time. We get distracted, and then we end up missing out on the information that is being transmitted, resulting in miscommunication and misunderstanding.

Practicing effective communication as a listener is all about understanding the message the speaker is trying to transmit to you. Agreeing with them isn't the goal here; you should instead simply desire to understand. Focus on your job, and make sure that what the speaker intends to communicate is the message that you receive. When you're listening, your job is to listen, so do your best to not interrupt unless it's to ask for clarification about something the speaker has said. You should also do your best to avoid thinking about rebuttals or responses while you're listening, as this will distract you and stop you from listening intently. A great way to be an effective listener, especially in one-on-one conversations like a talk between you and your spouse, is to practice reflective listening. This is a process where as you listen, you provide the speaker with indications that you're listening such as positive and affirmative vocalizations, head nods, and a good level of eye contact. You can then 'reflect' back your understanding of what the speaker has said to them in order for them to make sure it matches the meaning of their original message.

Many people are of the opinion that they listen well to their spouse when in reality they only listen as far as they allow their spouse to speak. Rather than giving their partner as much time and space as they need to express themselves, they will often take opportunities to cut them short to weigh in with their own opinion. Listening to your spouse when they talk is about validating their feelings regardless of whether you agree with how they feel about something. Your opinion on the matter is more or less irrelevant. It won't change how they feel. They feel how they feel, and the best way to work through difficult issues and troubling emotions is to simply let them feel it. You have to be patient, open and receptive to the way your spouse feels, no matter how you might feel about it. If they don't feel like you give them an open and non-judgmental forum for them to express themselves fully, they will only bottle up their emotions and end up resenting you. If listening hasn't been your strong suit in the past, make an effort to change that now by shutting up and paying attention to your spouse when they tell you how they feel. Encourage them to open up; tell them that you want to understand them better by just listening as they pour their heart out to you. Set aside any desire you may have to control how they feel or what they think or say. Simply let your partner be free to be themselves, and accept whatever they tell you without judgment and with an open mind. Be patient by allowing them to speak with complete freedom and at their own pace.

Learning to listen to your spouse properly represents a quantum leap in your relationship and marriage. By giving them space and time to fully express themselves, they will probably be motivated to reciprocate and return the favor for you. Establishing a culture of openness, freedom of expression, and emotional security in your marriage in this way lays the groundwork for dealing with past, current, and future problems alike in a way that is mature, calm, and empathetic. Listening to people helps you to understand them better. The reasons they are the way they are, the little thoughts behind their actions, and the feelings behind their words become clearer. It helps you to genuinely put yourself in their shoes and see things from their perspective, a skill that might as well be a superpower when it comes to managing your relationships with people. Listening might not be the single key to saving your marriage, but it's an important first step.

Body Language

When it comes to face-to-face communication, many people tend to assume that speaking and listening makes up the bulk of it. In fact, the majority of communication in interpersonal interaction is nonverbal. Some researchers and behavioral psychologists even think it might be as much as 90%! When we speak or even listen, we're not talking only with our words. Our bodies automatically broadcast messages about how we feel and what we think. This is a mostly subconscious process, although we can control it when we pay attention to it for as long as we pay attention to it — much like breathing. On the whole, however, our body language is something that happens without us even noticing we're doing it, meaning it can often betray our true feelings when we're trying our best to put on a front with our words.

These subtle indicators of our true internal feelings manifest themselves in a variety of ways; our posture, the way we carry and hold ourselves, what we do with our hands or our legs, and our facial expressions all give clues to what state of mind we're in and how we feel about a particular situation. For example, having our arms crossed is defensive body language, and suggests a person feels uncomfortable or on edge. Likewise, having our hands by our sides or using them animatedly when we're speaking suggests a more open and expressive mood. Additionally, our tone of voice and eye contact also give away signs of our internal makeup. Our body language is usually interpreted by others on a subconscious and automatic level. While it's not something we tend to notice or think about consciously, our minds nevertheless pick up on it and note what another person's body language is broadcasting. This manifests itself as a gut feeling we get about someone; we can pick up on when someone is angry or upset relatively easily, just because of the body language they're giving off — although we might not even think about how we know.

Body language is a very instinctual and primitive form of communication. It's what most animals rely on to communicate in the wild, even ones with complex social groups and complicated interactions such as our fellow great apes or dogs and cats. Although we might like to think of ourselves as highly evolved and educated, relying on our words rather than our bodies, we're still highly tuned in and sensitive to body language. We not only pick up on the body language of other people, but we trust what it's telling us more than we trust the words they're saying. This is why we can pick up on sarcasm pretty easily. When the message of someone's words doesn't match their tone of voice or their body language, we disregard the words and use their behavior and tone to judge their true feelings. We also tend to mirror other people's body language when we're interacting with or otherwise paying attention to them, without noticing we're doing it. Next time you're in a group meeting, cross your arms and lean back in your chair, and then notice other people doing it too over the next few minutes. Mirroring body language in this way is an instinctive way of promoting social cohesion and synchronizing mood in order for us to better fit in with the people around us.

Mirroring can also be reverse engineered in a way to read what another person's body is saying. When you notice someone's body language but are struggling to work out what it's saying about their inner being, you can mimic it at a later point when you're alone and see what kind of feelings a certain behavior gives you. Through doing this, you can try to grasp what another person's body language was saying about themselves. You can also take advantage of this innate and unconscious form of communication to improve the way you communicate in your marriage. By noticing your spouse's body language and altering your behavior accordingly, you can respond to their mood in a more sensitive fashion. You can also try to broadcast more open and intimate body language so that your partner feels more relaxed and engaged with you.

When good communication breaks down and messages aren't being correctly transferred between you and your spouse, it can lead to real issues in your marriage. There are several causes of miscommunication and misunderstanding. Failing to listen with full attention or using poorly chosen words are some of the biggest culprits of this. A real limitation of communication is that it depends on individual interpretation. In order to understand a message, we have to interpret it by comparing and contrasting it to things we already understand. This is essentially how the brain processes information — through association. This means that people can have very different interpretations of the same message, simply because they have different sets of associations in their mind that are triggered when they hear certain words or phrases. The connotations and inferred meaning of any one message can vary greatly from person to person. For example, one person may love dogs and positively receive communication from someone talking about dogs, a person with a fear of dogs may receive the exact same communication in a very different and much more negative manner. Your communication is therefore limited by yours and your audience's ability to process and understand what is being said. Accommodating for and overcoming these differences when it comes to your marriage involves speaking often and at length, to gain a better understanding of your spouse's communication style.

Chapter Two:
Making Marriage Work

There are times in every marriage when it feels like things are hopeless. Being with someone in such a close and personal way for such a prolonged period while under pressure from yourselves and others is a perfect storm for conflict, issues, and difficulty to brew up at certain points throughout the course of your marriage. In this chapter, we'll be looking at what both you and your spouse have to do to make things work and get your marriage back on track and headed in the right direction.

Attitude, Mindset, and Perspective

As I indicated in the previous chapter, every marriage has roughly the same amount of unresolvable problems, whether it's a great marriage or a terrible one. What this tells us is that making your marriage not only work but be a beautiful and fulfilling experience for both you and your partner all comes down to the way the two of you perceive it and how you view each other. The attitude you have towards your marriage is the most important determining factor in the actual content and quality of the marriage itself.

The reason for this is that attitude and perspective shape everything in our lives. At the end of the day, things being good, bad, or somewhere between is simply a matter of how you choose to view things. Marriage is no different. Regardless of the actual objective quality of your marriage, the way you view it determines whether it is positive or negative. In fact, objectively. your marriage doesn't even exist, save for words on paper. It's a concept; it's subjective. What it is, is what you and your spouse view it as and therefore determine it to be.

This can be a difficult idea to wrap your head around at first, so stay with me here. I promise that if you can get to grips with this, everything else about your marriage will eventually fall into place. Your marriage is what it is; it could always be better, it could always be worse. No marriage or relationship is perfect. It's simply the nature of being human. If you decide to focus on the positive aspects of your marriage first, your marriage will seem a more positive thing in your mind. You will approach your spouse in a more upbeat and friendly way. You will be more grateful for all of the good things your marriage represents. Not that you should neglect the negative aspects of your marriage or ignore them completely — on the contrary, you should always seek to resolve issues wherever you can, learn from them, and then move on — but whether you focus on the positive or negative aspects of your relationship is a choice that you can and do make, every second of every day. Every thought you have or word you speak to your partner is either positive or negative in context. It either comes from a place of love or a place of hate. If you make the constant decision to try to view your marriage in a more positive light, in a more loving and grateful and appreciative way, it will become more positive over time. When both you and your spouse commit to trying to see the good in your marriage rather than dwelling on the bad, incredible things are possible. Attitude is the key to restarting your relationship, recalibrating your mind, and refocusing your attention on all of the beautiful things your marriage stands for.

In exactly the same way, it can alter your mindset towards conflict and issues in order for these unavoidable obstacles to appear in a more positive light. A marriage is about a bond between you and your spouse. The two of you are a team, even when it doesn't feel like it. You need to have each other's backs through thick and thin. It should be 'me and you versus the problem' rather than 'me versus you', every time. This first attitude promotes teamwork and working together to overcome obstacles as a unit. The latter does nothing but breed resentment. It doesn't matter who's to blame; we're all to blame for something, sooner or later. What's really important is being able to sit down and work out how to solve an issue rather than worrying about who's right and who's wrong.

Making a marriage work requires total commitment to the journey, no matter where it might take you. There will be difficulties, of course, but there always are in life. There's no way to avoid it; it's the way things are. Having a perfect, frictionless relationship or marriage isn't possible and should never be your goal. Instead, you should seek to be able to deal with issues in an emotionally healthy and productive way when they come up, rather than lapsing into shouting matches or blaming each other. Respect, honesty, trust, and effort are the cornerstones of any marriage, and making sure all four of these are present in both you and your spouse's minds is essential to making things work.

Often, marriages fall apart because things get stale. Once the honeymoon period has worn off and the flames of infatuation have died down a bit, people tend to feel like they have lost the passion somewhere along the way. They might feel less excited about their spouse or grow used to them being there and start to crave the tension and excitement of a new relationship. The beginning of a relationship is characterized by chemicals such as dopamine being released in both your brain and that of your partner. This is why relationships feel so exciting at first — there's a rush of chemicals in your brain that makes you feel incredible. Lots of people get hooked on this feeling, going from relationship to relationship to get their next hit of dopamine and ride the high of a new romance. Others make the mistake of equating this feeling with love. Once they've been with someone for a while, especially after marriage, the flames tend to die down and the chemicals that cause this feeling wear off and stop being released in such high doses; they feel like something's changed, like the love has worn off. This isn't the case, however. The love hasn't gone anywhere, because the feelings they felt before weren't love. It was just the rush from of bonding chemicals that come from a new relationship.

What is love, then, if not that feeling? That's a question that even philosophers have grappled with and struggled to answer. In my view, love is something far deeper than the shallow feelings caused by chemicals in your brain when you first start hooking up with someone new. Love is a choice; it's an attitude. It's the decision to treat your partner well because you care about them and want them to be happy. It's something much deeper and more fulfilling than any dopamine rush could ever be. It's the smoldering, glowing heat that's left once all the flames have died down — and it burns much, much hotter than any flame ever could. This is the reality of human romantic relationships. It doesn't matter who you're with, eventually, the flames of infatuation will subside, and you're left with something beautiful and enduring. This doesn't mean the passion has to leave your marriage, however. Things only get stale if you neglect the relationship and allow them to get stale. You can stoke the fire and add more fuel by putting in the effort to keep things fresh and spice it up. You never know all there is to know about a person, no matter how long you've been with them. If you keep up a desire to continuously learn about your spouse and remain excited to explore life together, you'll always feel close to them and passionate about being with them.

Expectations

An important part of getting your attitude and mindset right when it comes to your marriage is to have a healthy perspective on things by managing your expectations. Everyone has different preferences and different ideas about how things should be. People are independent and autonomous, and what appeals to one half of a married couple might not appeal to the other. This is not a bad thing, it's just another part of being human. Disappointment occurs when the reality of a situation fails to live up to the expectation we had of it beforehand. This can lead to a multitude of issues, both small and large, within the context of a long-term relationship or marriage.

A common result of mismanaged expectations is one partner feeling like they just aren't good enough for their spouse. They feel constantly criticized and critiqued, as though they're always being assessed and can't ever do enough to please their other half or meet their expectations. The result of this is that they always feel on edge and unable to relax around their partner for fear of doing something they judge to be 'wrong' or unacceptable. No relationship should feel this way; certainly not a marriage. Being married to someone should mean you're able to feel totally relaxed and at home when you're together, not like you're on parole.

The solution to a situation like this is two-fold. While constant criticism is abrasive and undermines a relationship because it forms a pattern of consistent negative behavior, it's often about relatively insignificant individual circumstances grouped together over a period of time. This makes it easy to overreact, particularly when it feels like it's never ending. A slight snide remark or sarcastic comment can be the straw that breaks the camel's back. With this in mind, whenever you find yourself on the receiving end of your partner's unrealistic expectations, take a deep breath and try to remain calm. Your fight-

or-flight response has been triggered because of what you perceive to be a threat to your happiness, ego, or self-esteem. When this response is active, your prefrontal cortex — the part of your brain responsible for reasoning, evaluation, and rational thought — isn't able to function normally. This reduction in your ability to think logically can make you snap and overreact, causing the situation to rapidly spiral out of control.

Healthy communication about what each person expects from themselves, each other, and the marriage is necessary to set things straight and avoid future conflict. The best time to do this is early on in the relationship, and the second best time is right now. If you don't talk openly about what you need, want, and expect from your marriage, how is your spouse supposed to understand what they need to do in order for the both of you to be happy? Your job is to love each other and try your best to understand one another. When we understand each other better, we become less irritated by each other, and this is only possible through open and honest communication about our expectations.

Dealing With Bitterness And Resentment

These two things characterize every dysfunctional, unhappy marriage. The negative experiences we have with our spouses lead to us becoming jaded and withdrawn, holding grudges against each other and wishing that they would change. Conflict leads to defensiveness, reaction, overreaction and contempt on both sides. Communication becomes difficult, and communication about difficult issues becomes all but impossible. Under these circumstances, maintaining a healthy and fulfilling marriage seems like a pipe dream. We begin to stonewall one another, withdrawing emotionally from the relationship we have with our spouses and meeting any attempts at reconciliation with defensiveness and skepticism. When we grow to resent the people we love the most, it feels like there's too much bad blood to ever go back to the way things were. Too much has changed. Every interaction feels like it has a dark cloud hanging over it. We become so sick and tired of being hurt that we begin to expect it at every turn, so we become openly hostile to stop ourselves from having to experience the agony of being hurt any more.

The thing is, the current reality of our relationships and marriages are not decided by what has happened in the past, but by the attitude we bring to them now. If we decide to bring a negative attitude shaped by the bad experiences we've had before, our current reality will be negative, too. We always have a choice when we interact with someone else; we treat them in a way that stems from a place of love or a place of hate. If we're going to make things work with any one person, we have to choose to treat them with love, kindness, and compassion in the present moment, regardless of their actions in the past or present. Ask yourself, 'what kind of person do I want to be? What kind of marriage do I want to have?' The way you treat and think about your spouse shapes the quality of the relationship that you have with them. Making it work means making a commitment to leave bitterness and resentment behind and move on.

Positive, healthy communication based on the correct principles and coming from the right place is essential to moving past the difficulties we experience in marriage. You've loved each other enough to choose to get married, so you need to make a decision to treat each other with love and kindness now. Throughout my years as a therapist, I've heard countless married couples tell me that they hate and despise each other. And yet, in my experience, this isn't true the vast majority of the time, even if they think it is. It isn't possible to feel strong hate for something unless you blame it for causing the loss of something you love. Almost all of the couples who claimed to hate each other were simply grieving for the love they'd once had and lost and blamed each other for ruining. The love was still there underneath; it never went away. All they needed to do was to learn to see things from a different perspective. To put their egos aside, commit to making things work, and then work together to overcome their problems. Hate is always a reaction to hurt. When we're hurting, we lash out and we hurt the people we love, who in turn hurt and hate us out of the hurt they're experiencing. This is just another unfortunate aspect of the human condition. When we feel threatened or cornered, such as when we're forced into a difficult conversation we're not ready to have, we lash out. Sometimes people lash out and there's no apparent cause — whatever it is, it's hidden. Their behavior is simply a manifestation of whatever has caused them hurt, whether it's something you've done or something totally unrelated to the relationship that you have with them.

When you decide to choose love, to put the bitterness and resentment aside and focus on reconnecting emotionally with your partner, your relationship will change before your very eyes. You'll find you become more observant and grateful for the good things about your spouse and your marriage. There's power in gratitude; being grateful for things changes your outlook and perspective on your relationship. If you communicate this gratitude to your spouse, your relationship will begin to thaw, no matter how frosty things might be. Choosing love is about communicating the value you place on your relationship and on your spouse to them. Appreciate your spouse and tell them why. You can do this in any number of sweet and thoughtful ways that allow you to demonstrate what they mean to you. You can leave sweet messages for them on the refrigerator or in their lunch, or come home early from work just to spend time with them. Let them know that your life is better because they're in it.

Change the energy of your relationship in order to influence the perception that you and your partner have of it and of each other. Avoid criticism wherever you can, particularly if it's over something trivial, and where you can't avoid it, be kind, compassionate, loving, and tactful in your criticism. Bear in mind that criticism doesn't have to be intended or even real in order to have negative effects on your marriage — it only has to be perceived. Try to change the way you interact with your partner to come from a place of love, rather than a place of indifference or negativity and hate. Change your mindset towards your marriage, and most importantly change the way you deal with problems. Remember, it's the two of you against the problem, every time, regardless of what the problem is. Respect each other as allies and friends as well as partners. Focus on being positive and bringing positivity into your marriage, no matter how much of an uphill battle that might appear to be at first. The hardest part of these things is always getting started. Act and speak as often as you can from a place of compassion, kindness, patience, and understanding. Love is an effort, and you have to put in as much of it as you can to put the resentment behind you.

Most importantly, you have to be able to forgive. Forgiveness is no easy feat. It will take all the patience and understanding you're able to muster. It might help to remember that things rarely turn out the way we want or plan them to. Things simply unfold, and we sometimes find ourselves in situations where there's no easy way out. You're in this together, and no matter what might have happened in the past, if both of you regret any wrongdoing and mistakes and want to push on together towards a better future, it doesn't matter. I've had many clients over the years who believed that their marriage was on life support and well past making a healthy recovery. Too much had happened; there were too many bad feelings, too many lies, too much infidelity, and resentment and ill-feeling. In almost every case, their marriage wasn't past repair, no matter how badly damaged it might have been. As I've said before, the circumstances don't matter. I've seen it all. The only thing that really matters when it comes to marriage, in the end, is the willingness to try to make things work. That alone can overcome any number of problems.

What Destroys A Marriage?

Everybody has different ideas about what causes divorce. Every divorce results from its own unique story of hurt and misery. The one thing that rings true through virtually every destroyed marriage I've experienced in my career is that ultimately, most of the pain we feel isn't caused by other people but comes from within ourselves. It's not out there, it's not caused by the people or the circumstances in your life; ultimately, it's inside you. Most people fail to realize this and stay married and miserable because of it. They blame others for their problems but deep down they know that they'd be unhappy no matter who they were with.

You can stay married, but you don't have to stay miserable. Leaving someone or getting a divorce is no guarantee of happiness, anyway. It won't take away the pain or emptiness that's inside us. Our subconscious minds rule us. We're programmed to act in the way we act. This is something we don't like to admit to ourselves. Everyone likes to believe that they're acting of their own free will. The truth is, we're wired to be the way we are by our genetics and the way we've been shaped by the things that happened to us in life, particularly in childhood. We tend to treat our husbands and wives the way we witnessed our parents treating each other while we were growing up. The things we're exposed to as children serve as templates on which we model our behavior as adults without even realizing it. This process is known as 'imprinting'. It shapes everything about our future selves, from our loyalties and standards to our behavior. Some people are programmed by this process to be 'leavers,' while others are programmed to want to stay. We're programmed to meet conflict by either shutting down or flaring up with anger. Patterns that are formed in childhood can, therefore, end up destroying marriages as adults.

This is particularly true for those of us who were victims of physical or emotional abuse in our childhood. Abuse, neglect, and abandonment all leave deep and lasting scars, terrible pain inside that we struggle to process. This then affects our marriages later in life when the programming is triggered and resurfaces. We then find ourselves caught in a tornado of pain and misery that sweeps away all of the people and things that we love and that are important to us. Becoming aware of our programming and talking about our childhood experiences with our spouse helps us to deal with the pain inside and overcome our childhood programming. Communication is the key, not pushing the one we love away from us out of pain and fear. Most marriages are destroyed from the inside out, not from the outside in. Fortifying the bond you have with your spouse through positive and open communication about difficult emotional issues can help the two of you to help each other through difficult times and stay together.

Improving Your Marriage

When it comes to improving the quality of your marriage, you first need to embrace a paradox of sorts. The truth is that you don't really need to improve it as such; you just need to change how you perceive it. If you change the way you see your marriage, you'll make it a more positive thing to be a part of. The first step in making it better is to acknowledge that it's already good. If you scoff at this and believe your marriage is truly bad, I urge you to think again. The fact that you're reading or listening to this book in the first place suggests that you really want to try to save your marriage, so there must be something there worth saving. Even if you think your marriage is a negative thing overall, there will always be positive and redeeming aspects of it. Focus on these parts of your relationship with your spouse rather than the negative things.

Simply put, your marriage is what it is — it can always be better, and it can always be worse. You're wired to judge and evaluate everything in your life, so try to judge your relationship in a certain way. Rather than always telling each other and yourself how bad things are, try instead to think and talk about how good it is. Your reality is whatever you pay attention to, so pay attention to all the good things about your spouse. Document the ways your marriage is a great thing to be a part of and appreciate and enjoy them. Show your spouse what they mean to you, and your marriage will begin to improve.

Developing an Action Plan to Make Your Marriage Work

An effective way of implementing real, lasting change in your marriage is to develop an action plan. This is a structured, formulaic way of approaching your marriage, meaning you can both agree upon it and then go ahead and work on it together while charting your progress. One of the best ways I've found to put this method into action is to sit down together and draw up a list of all the steps you want to take as a couple to get your marriage back and track and make progress together. These should be tailored to your specific situation and can be anything that the two of you need to do to make things work, as long as you can both do them together.

The first thing you need to do is make a list of all the areas of conflict and disagreement in your marriage. From this, you can then work out what you need to do to make your action plan work for your marriage. I'd also recommend considering the following 12 steps when drawing up your plan:

1. **Focus on yourself:** You can't control the actions of anyone other than yourself — not even your spouse. All you can do is work on yourself and hold up your half of the action plan. If your spouse is struggling, then you should be there to support them, but you can't work on them or change them from the

outside. Lasting change always comes from within.

2. **Learn to express concerns positively:** This is also known as constructive criticism. Part of being a good spouse and a good friend to someone is to be there to tell them the uncomfortable truths that they might not want to hear. While it's your job to express your concerns, you don't have to be spiteful about it. Think about how you can phrase things to your spouse when you're bringing up an issue to give them a more positive, supportive, constructive spin on the problem. This will help them deal with the issues they're facing in a much healthier way, rather than feeling like you're just being overly critical and petty.

3. **Commit to making decisions together:** When you're married, the two of you are a

team. The things you do affect each other in a very personal and direct way. As such, it's only right that you should make big decisions together, because your spouse deserves to have a say in decisions that will affect them as well as you. Additionally, consider that your spouse should represent the most intimate and well-developed relationship you have in your life. A healthy marriage is one where each person seeks each other's advice and counsel because they respect one another's opinions.

4. **Work on your energy:** Through your actions, words, and attitude, you bring a certain energy and intensity to your marriage. You can control and shape this energy to focus it in different areas and into different moods. You can and should work to improve the type and amount of energy you bring to your marriage to try to make it as

positive as possible. While it's not healthy to fake how you feel or pretend that you're fine when you're not just for the sake of your spouse, you can influence how you feel by paying attention to the right things. You should try your best to keep your energy positive by focusing on the good things in your life and marriage, rather than paying attention to all of the negative aspects of your life.

5. **Speak openly and often:** Communicate, communicate, communicate. You need to talk to your spouse frequently, and the quality of the communication needs to be as high as possible. While you don't have to be glued at the hip to your spouse, find and take all opportunities to talk that you can. Remember to try to listen more than you speak, and when you speak, speak from the heart. Be open about how you feel and what

you think. Try to stick to your word by meaning what you say; this is known as having integrity and will make your marriage a thousand times better.

6. **Trust each other:** Trust is the bedrock that relationships are built on. Without it, being married is like trying to construct a cathedral on foundations made of sand; it just can't be done. The whole thing implodes and sinks in on itself before long. Trust has to be earned, it's true, but trust also has to be given to make things work. You have to accept the fact that some people will hurt you in life, and that all you can do is trust the ones you love; the rest is up to them. Some would go even further and say that everybody hurts you eventually. Part of learning to love your life is working out who is worth hurting for. If there are serious reasons for a deep lack of trust in your relationship, we'll be going over

how to work on rebuilding it in the fourth chapter of this book, no matter how bad it gets — so hang in there.

7. **Show gratitude and appreciation:** There are few things more exhausting than working hard and trying your best only to feel underappreciated and unacknowledged for your effort. Cultivating a happier, healthier marriage is only possible if you're able to recognize your spouse's loving actions and support by sincerely thanking them and telling them that you appreciate them for everything they do.

8. **Show emotion:** No matter how foreign it might feel to wear your heart on your sleeve and put your emotions on show, it's an important part of being human and being in a loving relationship. You're not a rock. Your someone's husband or wife. You're a human

being, and you feel emotion. That's a beautiful thing. Without emotion, life would be meaningless. Embrace the full spectrum of your life and show and tell your spouse how you feel. When you're excited, when you're happy, when you're sad: it doesn't matter. Be yourself, be open, and show them how you really feel inside rather than keeping those feelings to yourself.

9. **Be honest:** Total honesty can be a very bitter and difficult pill to swallow, but if you genuinely want to forge a marriage that lasts and is full of loving and happy memories when you look back on it at the end of your life, it's essential. You absolutely have to be honest with your spouse, no matter how hard it is. You have to have the humility to hold your hands up and admit when you're wrong. You have to be grounded enough to admit your mistakes and seek forgiveness.

Nothing else will do. Without honesty, a marriage can never go the distance. No matter how good you might be at keeping things to yourself, something will slip eventually. Your spouse will find out what it is that you don't want them to know, and it will break the trust in your relationship. If you really want to make things work, then work on being honest.

10. **Support and respect:** Your job as a spouse and a partner is to be there for your other half through thick and thin. You need to be their rock when times are hard and they need to return the favor for you when it's your turn to need a shoulder to cry on. You support, uplift, and encourage each other not from a sense of duty but from mutual respect that transcends everything else. You love each other. You're on the same team: your team. No one else comes close;

it's the two of you. So be there for each other, and never sell each other out. If you can't rely on your spouse to have your back when the chips are down, then who can you rely on?

11. **Touch often:** True intimacy and genuine emotional closeness aren't possible without physical contact. Once this dwindles in a marriage, people begin to pull away from each other. Physical distance mirrors emotional distance. Increasing one will increase the other, and the reverse is also true. When you're not touching each other in a loving and affectionate way on a regular basis, you will begin to grow apart. You have to reintroduce frequent and extended periods of physical contact to reconnect with your spouse and improve your marriage. Small things like holding hands and cuddling

are just as important as having sex and kissing each other on the cheek.

12. **Make the effort:** No relationship can last when one or both halves of the couple aren't putting in the effort, and marriage is no different. Just because you're legally bound to one another doesn't mean that you can just kick back and relax your standards without the bond you have suffering. Work hard to make your spouse feel special and loved. Have fun with each other. Don't let the passion wilt. Go out on dates. Be spontaneous. Do things you've never done before and do them together. Life is short and you're with each other because you love each other. Embrace life with your best friend. Have fun.

Chapter Three:
Dealing With Porn Addiction

This topic is such a common issue now in the information age with everyone having access to the internet, I've dedicated a whole chapter to it. Porn addiction is a particularly tricky subject to deal with, both because the intimate and private nature of masturbation means it can be embarrassing and difficult to talk about and because many people suffering from it struggle to admit that they have a problem, even to themselves.

Porn and the Brain

In order to address how to deal with a porn addiction, we first have to look at the background surrounding what porn does to a person's brain and why it can be so damaging and so difficult to deal with. Contrary to popular belief, both men and women can suffer from an addiction to porn, although it's true that men tend to be more prone and vulnerable to it. This is because of the biological differences in how men and women perceive and react to sex and sexual stimuli. By and large, men are attracted to and focus on the physical aspects of women. This results from evolutionary biology; we're programmed to want to reproduce (or, at least, to do the things that fulfill our drive and cause us to reproduce). It's in our DNA, coded into us over millions and millions of years of evolution. However, there are stark biological differences in the way that men and women reproduce that influence our behavior when it comes to sex.

First, men have no way to guarantee that offspring is theirs (in an evolutionary context, disregarding modern science, of course). This is in contrast to women, who have to grow, carry, and give birth to a baby. They have total parental certainty; they have successfully passed their genes on. The result of this is that in order for men to make sure that they have passed on their genes, they have to rely on putting their eggs in as many baskets as possible, so to speak. They're genetically coded to want to diversify, to spread their sperm around in order to toy ensure that at least some women carry their children for them. This means that they're naturally prone to want to sleep with as many women as possible. They're attracted to all of the things that signal to them that a woman is fertile, healthy, and likely able to bear their children; such as wide 'child-bearing' hips. This makes porn particularly appealing to men. The dominantly visual aspect of it presses all of their evolutionary buttons. The same isn't necessarily true for women. Since they don't have to worry about the uncertainty of passing on their genes, they tend to instead seek men who will provide the resources they need to look after their child and make sure of their reproductive success by helping their offspring to survive and reach adulthood. Women tend to, therefore, be more attracted to things that indicate a suitable partner; such as personality, intelligence, and the ability to provide resources. Women tend to be less attracted to men's bodies and more attracted to the role that a man can play for them; sex is therefore usually a more emotional attraction for women.

Setting this aside for a minute, we now must look at what porn does to our brains. In order to do this, we have to think about the context of modern technology and how it can present us with very different circumstances than we've evolved to experience. Men are programmed to seek variety and novelty in order to maximize their chances of reproductive success. With online pornography, they can see more women in a sexual context in a short period of browsing than their ancestors would have been lucky to see in a lifetime. Men's brains tend to be more prone to being hijacked by porn because it temporarily satisfies a very primal and unscratchable itch. Porn can totally carry away the pleasure center of their brains with nearly limitless fulfillment and will cause a person to seek to indulge in it as often as they can.

Part of the reason porn is so addictive relates to the biological, chemical nature of our brains. Porn and masturbation stimulate dopamine release. We get addicted to the chemical kick that results from doing these things. This kick is a very short but intense one, not unlike incredibly addictive drugs like crack cocaine. This can make people constantly crave it or have it on their mind at all times, with an urge so overwhelmingly powerful it turns into a compulsion many people find themselves powerless to resist. This can have serious consequences for a person's sex life, particularly if they're married. Porn offers a very direct, convenient, visually satisfying, novelty-indulging, erotic stimuli that sex in the real world just can't live up to. This can affect a marriage or relationship due to the differences in expectation over the sex life of the couple. For example, a wife may feel neglected and overlooked because her husband gets all of his kicks from porn instead of having sex with her. To the porn user, sex just isn't as fulfilling or gratifying as their addiction, and so it wins every time.

Another aspect of porn addiction that needs to be addressed is that a person can become desensitized to sex in a number of ways. First of all, the novelty, variety, and convenience they've come to crave and expect to be sexually fulfilled just isn't there. Secondly, because they've become accustomed to a certain amount, type, and frequency of stimulation from masturbation, some people, especially men, can find it very hard to climax from sex alone. Neither of these side effects are particularly conducive to a mutually fulfilling sex life for a married couple.

Overcoming Porn Addiction

In order to overcome a porn addiction, it's important for a sufferer to first understand the operating equipment of their own mind. They can use this knowledge to deconstruct the process that is happening in their mind when they feel the urge to watch porn. The first thing that needs to be kept in mind is the nature of the problem: a person with a porn addiction isn't the problem. They aren't somehow a more flawed or a worse person than anyone else. Any addiction or compulsion is perpetuated by itself; the more it is indulged, the more entrenched it becomes and the harder it is to kick. Every time a person watches porn and masturbates to get the reward, the more conditioned they become to associate porn with sexual satisfaction. A chemical reaction is triggered, and they become addicted to the chemical rush in their brain. This makes it very difficult to deprogram themselves from the addiction; their brain is telling them to look after themselves because they have a need that can be taken care of. The only way to really overcome it is to break the vicious cycle of reinforcement that is sustained by indulging addictive, compulsive behavior such as watching porn and masturbating. Breaking this cycle can only be done through abstaining from the desire to watch porn.

Obviously, this is more easily said than done. Overcoming addiction involves rewiring your brain on a chemical and cognitive level. Luckily, because of the neuroplasticity of our grey matter, we can do this by changing our behavior. Porn is a purely psychological dependence, so when the behavior is changed, the dependence can be broken relatively simply, if not easily. Real and lasting changes in behavior have to come from within, from a person's desire to better themselves and have greater control over their biological urges, and from the willpower to wield a greater amount of influence over their own day-to-day lives. As is the case with trying to overcome any addictive behavior, relapse is inevitable. If accepting you have a problem is the first step to overcoming it, then accepting that you will relapse at some point and adopting an attitude of forgiveness towards yourself for it is the second.

Whenever we're faced with an addictive craving, we have to remember that we always have a choice as to how we act, even when it feels like we don't. We make the decision to indulge a behavior, rather than just failing to resist it. This is the harsh truth of any psychological addiction or dependency. However, when our brains are wired a certain way and we expect ourselves to indulge it, we often fall victim to it no matter how strong our willpower is. Despite this, you might find it helpful to mentally press the pause button when you feel the urge to watch porn and remember that you are going to decide what it is that you're about to do. Whether you make a positive or negative choice is up to you. You always have the opportunity to say no, to not indulge the behavior.

Distraction is a fundamental part of overcoming a porn addiction. When you feel the urge to watch it, resisting while remaining still mentally and physically turns it into a sheer battle of willpower. There's also something of a catch-22 involved here because the harder you try not to think of something, the harder it gets to not think about it. If you instead purposefully distract yourself, the craving will soon be forgotten and the urge to consume porn will subside. Some of the best forms of distraction are ones that involve doing something active mentally or physically in order to occupy your mind and body and take your thoughts away from porn. You could exercise by working out or going for a run or a walk, read a book, or even sit and quietly meditate by focusing on your breathing in order to calm your mind. Your end goal is simply to break the grip that pornography has over you by avoiding watching it or masturbating to it when you feel like you want to. If you can exert restraint and self-control over your actions on a regular basis and not give in to it, it's power over you will begin to slip and you will be able to reclaim control over your sex life. Porn is extremely powerful stuff, so it has to be used responsibly in order to avoid it becoming a serious problem in your life and marriage.

If your spouse is the one with the addiction to porn, then your job is to encourage and support them while trying your very best to be as understanding and non-invasive as possible. You need to understand that this situation is highly personal, and trying too hard to control your spouse's porn habits (and therefore sex life) will only lead to defensiveness on their part and more hostility between the two of you. Your role, just as much as the sufferer, is to understand the nature of the problem. Porn use tends to have moral implications for a lot of people, particularly religious folk, but it doesn't have anything to do with the quality of a person's character or their commitment to their marriage or family. The person isn't the problem; their brain chemistry is, and they can't help the way they're wired and that the internet and the porn industry exploits this. Instead of freaking out and overreacting and making out like it's the worst thing in the world, instead try to get some perspective.

Quick tip: Put yourself in your spouse's shoes and try to help them through empathy, rather than judging them. Don't make more or less of it than it is. It is what it is. Lots of people watch porn, and lots of people get addicted to it. How we perceive and respond to our addictions triggers our reaction to it. It can be easy for a person having their porn habits questioned to feel threatened and shut down completely, so try your best to be as sensitive as possible. The wrong approach may make the problem worse, particularly if you trigger your spouse's fight-or-flight response. Be loving, be forgiving, and be accepting. Remember to try and tackle the problem as a team, but remember that you can't control what anyone other than yourself does.

This is something your partner ultimately has to do alone, so just try to be there for them and provide a judgment-free forum for them to express themselves to you.

Chapter Four:
Rebuilding Broken Trust

As I've mentioned previously, trust is the foundation of any relationship. Once trust has been lost in a marriage, there's no going back to the way things were before. In this chapter, we'll examine why trust is so important, how it's broken, and how to rebuild it and your marriage after it's gone.

The Nature of Trust

Trust is a very strange concept, but it's one we're all intimately familiar with. It all stems from the nature of ourselves as human beings. We're vulnerable, finite creatures. We can be harmed, or taken advantage of, so we're safest when we have friends and allies; when we're in a group. We're highly social and tribal by nature, prone to surrounding ourselves with friends and family who all help to support each other so that we benefit mutually and have a better chance of survival. This emphasis on teamwork and cooperation means that we have to trust the people we're close with. If we don't trust, we can't let them be a true part of our lives, but when we trust, we give others the power to hurt us in some way.

Nowhere does this context of trust carry more weight than in a marriage. When we're married to someone, we're meant to be closer to them than to any other person we know. They are supposed to be our best friend and life partner, someone who always has our back, someone we can always rely on. They have the power to lift us up to heights that we didn't realise existed or tear us down. We give them the key to our hearts, and we have to trust that they mean what they say, that they love us as much as we love them and that they won't hurt us.

True trust has to be earned; it can't just be given away freely. It would take someone very naive to completely trust a stranger they'd just met. We have to demonstrate to others that we're good, trustworthy people if they're going to trust us at all. I like to think of trust like a savings account you might have with a bank. We have one of these accounts with each person we know, and everyone we know has one with us. When we do something that shows a person they can trust us, we make a deposit into this balance. If it's a small gesture, it might only be a small deposit. When we really help someone out or come to their aid in a time of need, especially without direct benefit to ourselves, these deposits can be much larger. Over time, these accounts grows considerably, with people we know well carrying a very high trust balance with us. When something happens that undermines that trust in some way, a withdrawal is made and the balance decreases; whether this is a large withdrawal or a small one depends on the context of the trust being undermined.

Infidelity and Lies

Every relationship and marriage will experience small withdrawals of trust sometimes. Everybody makes mistakes and handles situations badly, but most of the time these withdrawals are small and insignificant enough that once the problem is dealt with and motivations are explained, we deposit the withdrawn amount once more, perhaps even with a bit of interest. However, there are some things that can cause the trust in a marriage to be completely shattered, with virtually the entire balance withdrawn in one go. The two most common causes of trust being eroded quickly tend to go hand in hand with each other: infidelity and lies.

While not all lying in a marriage results from infidelity, virtually all instances of infidelity are followed by lies. Whether this means someone telling outright falsities to cover their tracks or simply lying by omission. Married couples will lie to each other about all kinds of things, however, and it always has negative consequences for their marriage one way or another. With the exception of innocent white lies, lying in any relationship slowly and insidiously erodes the trust that lies at the heart of it. Regardless of whether or not lies are exposed and revealed, they always have a corrosive and harmful effect on the relationship. When they are exposed, and a person realizes that their spouse has been lying to them, it brings up a whole host of other issues. If they were capable of lying about A, then who knows if they've been telling the truth about B through Z? Once the lying starts, it opens a can of worms. Unless the motivations for lying are explained, apologized, and taken responsibility for, it can lead to a slippery slope where the lied to partner doesn't know where to draw the line and continue to trust their spouse. When the lying goes unnoticed, it's only a matter of time. A lie that passes the first test and seems to go undetected is like an unexploded mine. It's only a matter of time before it's stepped on and blows up.

We tend to only lie to our spouses when we have something to hide and because we think that we have something to lose by telling the truth. This means that once a lie has been told about something significant, we have to lie again and again in order to cover our tracks and keep the original lie concealed. We have to maintain an awareness of what is a lie and what is truth to avoid our lying being discovered, which is an exhausting, draining exercise. As pathological liars know only too well, there comes a point after enough lying where you can no longer discern fact from fiction and lies simply become a part of what you come to think of as the truth. After all of this effort, a single slip and the whole story can come unraveled in one go, leaving the trust shattered and requiring a lot of communication and honesty to rebuild.

Nothing can break the trust in a marriage quite like infidelity and the lying that usually comes with it. Being faithful is a huge part of any monogamous relationship, and straying from your partner to hook up with someone else on the side can end even the strongest of marriages in one clean stroke. This is why so many of us try to cover up our mistakes when we've been unfaithful, although more lying only makes the problem worse when the very best thing to do is come clean. When a marriage has had problems with lying and/or infidelity, the trust has been broken, and the balance is withdrawn, it is possible to rebuild and save the marriage. It takes time, patience, forgiveness, and a lot of understanding, but it can be done.

Rebuilding Trust

The first thing that has to be understood about rebuilding trust is that when the trust in any relationship is seriously violated, there's no way to go back to how things were before. The dynamic has been changed for good. The old relationship is dead and gone; you have to start again from scratch. If the two of you can make things work, it will be in a new relationship, like a phoenix rising from the ashes of the old. Learning to trust someone again after they've let you down badly is a long and difficult journey. You might never be able to trust them again.

Whether or not it's possible to rebuild the trust in your marriage once it has been broken is a matter of context and your own values. What constitutes a dealbreaker to some people is more of a gray area for others. Some people see infidelity as the ultimate death knell or the final nail in the coffin, and won't let themselves remain married to someone who could betray them so badly, whereas others will do just about anything to make things work and stay together. My professional two cents on the matter is that context and circumstance are everything. If your spouse cheated on you once in a drunken mistake, owned up to it immediately, is ashamed of themselves for letting you down, and is dedicated to making things right, that's one thing. It's very saveable. If, however, your spouse has been involved in a pattern of cheating and lying, and shows no intention of owning up to what they've done or committing to becoming a better person and partner to you, then a very persuasive argument can be made that you'd be better off divorcing them and leaving them in the past. Keep in mind that these are two extremes; most instances of trust being badly broken aren't nearly as black and white, and contain varying amounts of lying and obstructing and dodging the truth. At the end of the day, only you are in a position to decide whether it's best to end your marriage for good or commit to trying to make it work.

Rebuilding Trust as the Perpetrator

Hurting the people we love is just another unfortunate aspect of being human. All too often, we hurt others because we're hurting ourselves, and we don't know how to deal with that pain in a way that is healthy. So we lash out, get ourselves into difficult situations, and end up bitterly regretting our actions when we realize what we've done. If you're the reason the trust has been broken in your marriage and you want to know what you need to do to get that back and reestablish a healthy relationship with your spouse, the first thing you need to do is forgive yourself — no matter how badly you want to hate and punish yourself.

Forgiveness is the path of healing that we can all choose to take at any time. Your spouse will have to forgive you in time, but that's not the most important thing right now. For them to forgive you and come to trust and respect you again, you have to first communicate openly and at length about what happened and why. This can't happen until you've begun the process of healing, and the first step on that long road is to forgive and understand yourself. Everybody makes mistakes. No one is perfect. True self-love comes from feeling ashamed, or guilty, or angry, or scared, and not resenting yourself for feeling that way.

Then you have to engage in a period of open conversation with your spouse about what has happened and why the trust between the two of you has been broken. You need to be completely honest with them, and they with you. The two of you need to work as a team to look at and address all the reasons your marriage got to this state in the first place, and how you're going to work on them going forward. It's not enough to simply commit to working on the symptoms. You have to reach the underlying causes and understand exactly what the flaws of your marriage are to put them right and carry out lasting change. Remember that trust has to be earned, not given freely, and that this is especially the case when that trust has already been broken. In fact, once you've broken someone's trust so fundamentally, they have every right to never believe a word you say ever again. 'Once bitten, twice shy' — you will need to demonstrate that you can be trusted and that you're committed to changing and to your marriage over and over again to help your spouse trust you even a little after everything that's happened. In all likelihood, you broke their heart. You must make deposits and avoid withdrawals over an extended period of time to really convince them that they can once again give you the power to break their heart.

In order to show your spouse that they can trust you again and that whatever happened was a mistake that won't ever be repeated, it's important that you are completely open and honest with them. You need to lay it all out on the table, no matter how difficult that might be, or how many more issues doing so might bring up. You owe it to them and to yourself to tell the full truth, no matter how painful it is. It goes without saying that if you've been involved in an affair, you need to end it. The best time was right before it started; the second best time is right now. Not only should you end the affair, but if you're committed to making your marriage work you should totally cut ties with the person you've been unfaithful with. That means deleting their number and erasing all traces of them from your life, including from your social media. Lots of people feel squeamish about doing this, particularly because they're worried about coming across as rude. Don't even factor being polite into doing what you need to do to stay with your spouse. This isn't the time to be concerned about being rude. It's time to save your marriage. So do what you need to do and trust that the other person will find their own way in life. You must expect and accept a period of total transparency; if your spouse requests to check your phone and social media, you'll either have to accept that this is the price of breaking and trying to rebuild trust or refuse and be kicked to the curb for having something to hide. Marriage is a highly intimate experience; we have to share sacred parts of ourselves with our partner. Losing an element of privacy is often the price you have to pay for breaking your spouse's trust. It's also important to say what you're going to do and then do what you say. You need integrity now more than ever if you're going to do what you can to help your spouse trust you again. The rest is up to them.

Rebuilding Trust as the Victim

When you've had the horrible experience of being on the receiving end of a trust-shattering blow to your marriage, it's tempting to pack up and call it a day then and there. No one would hold it against you if you decided that was what was for the best. However, all is not lost. There is still hope for your marriage. You can still be happy and fulfilled with the person you married. You can rebuild the trust you've lost and turn things around. It doesn't have to be over unless you decide it's over. If you're both willing to make it work, then there's no obstacle that you can't adapt to and overcome.

Once you've made the decision to work past a major breach of trust, there's a lot of difficult work ahead that you'll have to dive into and begin to work through. It will be a very tough process, but with perseverance, you will get there. I've seen all kinds of married couples in all kinds of horrible situations pull through and overcome the odds because, at the end of the day, attitude is the most important thing. You're not the first people to face the issues you're facing as a couple, and you won't be the first to overcome them. Couples have faced much, much worse and come out the other side stronger and better for it. I can assure you of that — I've witnessed it myself. If both you and your spouse are dedicated and committed to making things work, then the circumstances of the past don't matter, and they won't decide whether or not you end up being able to break new ground together. The only deciding factor is whether or not the two of you really want to make things work together.

The first thing you need to know when it comes to rebuilding trust is that the lack of trust isn't the primary problem your marriage faces, but rather a secondary problem. The primary problem is whatever broke that trust in the first place, and the fact that broken trust results from one of the principles of your relationship being violated. Trust issues result from something that has already happened that damaged that trust, and this is where you should focus your attention first, rather than on the matter of trust itself. The trust will return as a result of ensuring that you and your spouse are both clear on and dedicated to following the core principles of your relationship and your marriage.

Any relationship is based on certain principles that form the core of the bond between two people. What these principles are and how they're approached characterize every relationship, from great, loving, healthy, lasting marriages to abusive nightmares. Principles are also important in the wider context of your life, as the principles you stick to determine your life's outcomes. If you're going to rebuild the trust you've lost and learn how to make things work, then you need to work on how the two of you perceive and process the principles of your relationship. Before you do this, however, it's essential to understand the importance of positivity. The attitude with which you approach the whole task of rebuilding trust and mending your marriage will determine how successful you are in ultimately achieving this. If you try to maintain a positive outlook and an optimistic state of mind, you'll very likely be successful. If however, you focus on the negatives and don't truly believe that things can actually change for the better between you and your spouse, then you'll be trapped in a situation of your own making and that will be your reality. Your mindset matters. How you think will determine your outcomes.

Once you've adopted the right attitude, you need to examine the principles and values of your marriage. These are the 'why' behind your entire relationship with your spouse; the shared sense of purpose you both possess. Many people won't examine these at all throughout the course of their marriage. Sometimes people end up forgetting why they're even together in the first place. Naturally, these vary from marriage to marriage, so you'll have to look at those things that make yours unique and work out where you both stand on them. Some of the most important ones in any relationship are:

1. **Humility:** This is when you don't put your own wants and needs above those of other people because you have a humble view of your own importance and realize that you're no better than anyone else just because you're you. It represents openness and a willingness to change, and is essential to making any marriage work. Too often, we believe that we are 100% right, and as a

result we treat each other horribly. It's important to be able to put your own ego aside and acknowledge that who is right or wrong isn't important; working together is.

2. **Forgiveness:** This is the ability to leave the past in the past, to give up any demands that what has happened before be any different to how it has played out now, and move on from hurt and resentment. At the end of the day, stuff happens in life. Everybody makes mistakes. If we aren't able to forgive, we live our whole lives miserable and holding grudges against the people we think have wronged us, as well as against ourselves.

3. **Respect** - Being a respectful person is an integral part of remaining happily married and making your marriage a success. It isn't just about treating your spouse respectfully, though. How you treat those around you and

the people you interact with on a day-to-day basis — especially the people who can't do anything for you — says a lot about who you are as a person. Respect isn't just about respecting those that respect you, or respecting people only when they treat you with respect. The true measure of a person's character is if they can be respectful towards everyone, regardless of whether or not that respect is reciprocated.

4. **Love:** This may seem like an obvious inclusion, but many people seem to assume that love is something that just comes naturally, as though it's simply a force of nature. This may be at least partly true, but in order to really love you have to make choices. Being married presents you with many different opportunities to make choices and decisions. You can always choose to love, and you have to make the

decision to love your spouse every day of your life, no matter what. The two of you have to choose to love each other, to stick by each other even when times get tough and things get hard.

5. **Compassion and kindness:** Being married means you are someone's best friend and life partner. You should try your hardest to cultivate all of the love and compassion you possibly can for yourself and for your spouse, for both of your sakes. These two things go hand in hand and are like an infinite spring inside of you. The more you embrace these values and make them a part of your life and your marriage, the more you will feel their effects on your own mindstate and life. The more kindness and compassion you treat your spouse with, the more you will receive from them in turn.

6. **Work:** When it's all said and done, marriages require hard work — lots of it. The default trajectory of any relationship left to its own devices is down. In order to elevate the trajectory of your marriage and keep on moving onwards and upwards, you need to put in the effort. You need to try, and you need to want to succeed at the endeavor of being married.

If you and your spouse apply the right principles to your marriage and commit to working through problems together, you can rebuild any broken trust with time. Although it may be difficult to believe in the aftermath of a significant breach of trust, with enough hard work you can come out on the other side of it with a stronger marriage and a better understanding of each other than you had before the trust was lost. You can be happier, healthier, and more satisfied together than you ever imagined was possible by sticking together and pulling through when the chips are down. You can use the broken trust as the catalyst that propels your marriage to new heights, to heal and strengthen it and prevent such occurrences from ever happening again.

A point that I think is worth making here is that no matter how tempting it might seem, you should not seek revenge on your spouse for anything they've done to you. I've had many clients over the years who expressed a desire to 'even the score' with their spouse, particularly in cases of infidelity. Most people don't follow through with these urges, but those who do inevitably regret it. In order for true healing and forgiveness to take place, the slate needs to be wiped clean. The past is the past. What's done is done. Your spouse can't take any of it back, although they might wish they could. If you're going to have any chance of making things work between the two of you, then you have to leave the infidelity, the lying, the resentment, and the petty desires for revenge in the past. Adding to that will only end up making the problem worse and muddying what might be the only chance you have of rebuilding the trust that is so vital to your marriage. Don't throw it all away just to get even — you'll only end up regretting it.

Perhaps the very best thing you can do to heal the wounds you have from having your trust broken is to talk about it. Express yourself. Share what happened with the people around you, the people you trust. Talk to your friends and family, or a therapist if you need someone impartial and professional. Talking about things helps us to work out what we think and how we feel about the things that happen to us. It helps us to get our heads around the problems we face and makes us feel more in control of the situation. However, there is something that you should try to keep in mind when it comes to talking to people about what has happened to you. When we're hurt and offended, we tend to create a story that we tell people in order to explain what has happened. While this is natural and beneficial in helping you to recover, take care not to make yourself out to be the victim. Even if you are totally blameless and the victim of circumstance and other people, it stops you from letting go. When we feel like the victim, we feel resentful and hard done by. This can stop you from being able to move on from the things that have happened because you're too hung up on being the helpless victim to allow yourself to let it go.

Quick tip: You should also make the time to communicate openly with your spouse. Not just about the breach of trust — although you will likely feel the need to talk to them at length and often about that - but also in terms of just enjoying each other's company. For healing to take place, you need to learn to view them as more than the person who so broke your trust. Your old relationship is gone, so take the time to forge a new one with them. Have fun getting to know each other again. Go on dates, just like you did when you first met, and broaden and deepen your understanding of one another through shared conversation, time, and experiences.

Chapter Five:
Dead Bedrooms

When we're young and idealistic, we tend to imagine that sex won't be a problem when we're married. It's easy to assume that when you're married to someone, sex is as frequent and as fulfilling as you could want it to be. While this may be true for some lucky people, for many others it's a bad joke. Millions of people are locked into sexless marriages where despite being married, they get less action than they would if they were single. This nightmarish scenario is all too common, horrible, and difficult to get out of, but it can be done. In this chapter, we'll be examining how.

Sex and Relationships

Sex is a vitally important part of any relationship. In fact, it's a vitally important part of being human. It's one of our most basic and powerful drives, second only to our desire to eat, drink, and sleep. There's a good reason for this: we are the result of millions upon millions of years of evolution where genes have been passed on from one generation to the next through sexual reproduction. If we didn't want sex as much as we do, we wouldn't be here in the first place. We're wired to want it, and we're wired to want it a lot. When we're not sexually fulfilled we don't just crave it, we need it; in a similar way to when we haven't eaten for a few days we're not just hungry, but famished. Sex drives and controls us far more than we might realize. We tend to pick out partners that we have sex with and become highly territorial over them. I'm sure everybody reading or listening to this book knows the acute feeling of jealousy we can get when we even imagine our sexual partner being with someone else instead of us. While relationships vary in style and type right across the world, most people in the west tend to seek and maintain monogamous relationships consisting of two people who are sexually exclusive. While choosing to have a different type of relationship to this is far from uncommon, the default for our western culture is that we pair up, settle down, and become exclusive.

Relationships and sexual satisfaction are therefore fundamentally linked. We rely on our partner to sexually satisfy us. With marriage, this link becomes even further cemented. Even when you're dating, differing libidos can cause couples to break up. It's not so easy to go back once you're married. You're locked in, relatively speaking, and if the sex dries up it isn't as simple as just up and leaving. Additionally, marriage itself seems to be the catalyst for the sex lives of come couples fading away. Why is it that unmarried couples don't seem to have so much of a problem with it when married couples suffer so badly?

The thing is, bad sex lives aren't only limited to marriages. There are plenty of unmarried couples out there who have less (or more!) sex than one or more partners would prefer. Generally speaking, however, people with bad sex lives as unmarried couples don't tend to get married, although when they do it's obvious that marriage isn't the reason for their lack of sex. Marriage itself can cause things to grow stale in the bedroom, however, and there are a number of reasons for this. For one thing, married couples tend to have known each other much longer than unmarried couples. This in itself can be a real problem for the sex life of any couple, because time breeds familiarity and routine and these things are the opposite of novelty, which, as we've already discussed, is a particularly big turn on for men; sex can become boring, predictable and stale simply due to the course of time taking the edge off of things. Sex by its very nature is a hormonal, exciting, spontaneous beast. It's opportunistic and heart-pounding in the wild. When you can set your watch by your marriage's sexual routine, it's no wonder that things start to seem dull. Another common cause of dead bedrooms in marriage is differences in the libido of each spouse. Contrary to what some may think, libidos aren't a rigid and unchanging description of a person's natural appetite to sex. They do tend to have a sort of default range that determines a person's sex drive, but this is prone to waxing and waning according to the circumstances and mindset of an individual throughout the course of their life.

A person's libido at any one point in their life can be influenced by a multitude of different factors. Stress from careers or financial pressure can make it very difficult to think about or focus on sex, or even to desire it in the first place. In the same way, body confidence issues, substance dependence, real or perceived time constraints, and feeling obliged or required to participate in sex can put people off of sex and result in a dead bedroom. Perhaps the single biggest factor for married couples in terms of the decline in the quantity and quality of sex they have is having children. Having kids is a game changer in a multitude of ways, but it can have an inordinate impact on the health of your sex life as a married couple. Having children can hit women especially hard due to the change in hormones that they experience during pregnancy and after birth. It isn't uncommon for women to lose interest in sex completely for a short period of time after they have a child, especially when the stress and pressure of having to look after a newborn and raise children is taken into account. Having children can also interfere in a couple's sex life in a practical way, as many couples are unwilling to shut their bedroom door in case their children want to come in and avoid making too much noise or letting things get too carried away in the moment to stop their children from overhearing.

In some marriages, another contributing factor to the lack of a healthy and fulfilling sex life is the issue of sex being used as a weapon or as a reward. When sex is withdrawn in order to punish or offered in order to persuade, it changes from being a mutually fulfilling and rewarding recreational and intimacy-boosting activity to being a commodity, used as a bargaining chip or withheld in order to curb unwanted behavior. This kind of sexual dynamic is incredibly unhealthy and breeds resentment in a marriage. Treating sex as a commodity changes the fundamental aspect of a relationship from one of togetherness and teamwork to one of conflict and contest. It tarnishes what should be a sacred and special act of intimacy and bonding, warping it into something to be used as a means to an end, rather than an end in and of itself.

Dead bedrooms can be disastrous for a marriage. Not only do the sex lives of our spouses suffer, but when there's a lack of sex there comes a lack of intimacy — and not just in the bedroom. Without sex, married couples drift apart. They become less physically and emotionally close, and can even begin to resemble housemates more than they do a romantic relationship. The cuddling stops. The holding hands and hugging and kissing each other on the cheek stops, and things can go downhill very quickly. Dead bedrooms tend to fuel a vicious cycle where the lack of intimacy and connection that result from the absence of sex makes it very difficult for a couple to reconnect and improve their love life. Once resentment and blaming each other sets in, a rift appears that can further separate a couple and drive them closer to divorce.

Restoring Intimacy in Your Marriage

Bringing a dead bedroom back to life is no easy task, and the most effective method is very much dependent on the problems of each individual marriage. Often, one of the biggest problems that dead bedrooms cause and perpetuate is that sex becomes a huge deal. It turns into the elephant in the room, a focal point and a key area of conflict with a lot riding on it. This can lead to the problem becoming far worse because both parties know it's a big deal and performance anxiety begins to set in.

Sex should be a mutually enjoyable activity that brings you and your spouse closer in your marriage and is shared and appreciated between you. A dead bedroom suggests that this is no longer the status of you and your spouse's sex life, but a lack of sex is more often the symptom of deeper problems in a marriage than it is a self-contained problem. Bringing the sex back so often involves working out what these issues are and addressing them first and foremost, before trying to tackle the issue of sex itself. More often than not, issues surrounding dead bedrooms tend to stem from a lack of good communication. If you can work to improve this by having open, honest, and patient conversations, both in general and on the topic of your sex life, then things should improve. Sort out the main flashpoints first, and with the lessening of conflict should come a thaw in the ice and improve intimacy. Work out the basics of why intimacy has been lost, and keep track of how much sex you're having as a couple in order to objectively assess the state of your sex life and have the difficult conversations necessary to rectify your problems.

You also need to work at creating a mutual desire for sex. It can be easy to classify yourself and your spouse into a high-libido and low-libido dichotomy and then blame each other for your differences in expectation of sex, but things are very rarely as simple as that. Your libido might influence how often you become aroused and desire sex with no prior stimuli, but it doesn't inhibit you from becoming aroused and desiring sex after it has been initiated. If, for example, you have a husband who has a low libido and rarely initiates sex; it doesn't necessarily follow that he doesn't enjoy or wouldn't like to have sex once you've initiated things — only that they don't think to initiate it themselves very often! There needs to be a frank and open discussion about your sex life as a couple, including the expectations each of you have about what your sex life should be like. Marriage is all about compromise, and you need to be able to meet in the middle. Perhaps one of you could be having sex slightly less often than you like, and the other could be having sex slightly more often than they might want. The result is that neither of you 'win' or 'lose'; you work together to come to a solution that works for both of you.

If you or your partner's low libido is an enduring problem, then it's wise to look at what the underlying causes of low libido might be. Perhaps it's a matter of self-esteem or poor self-image, or the taking of antidepressants, or emotional baggage that hasn't been dealt with properly. Whatever the underlying problem might be, working through it may help to improve libidos and enhance the sex life of your marriage.

Creating desire for sex also involves working harder on building up the atmosphere and tension surrounding it. Rather than being born out of a sense of expectation, routine, or duty, work to make sex a fun activity once again. Bring the excitement back! You can spice things up in any number of ways if you use a little bit of imagination. Try to cultivate an atmosphere of excitement and novelty surrounding your sex life by trying new things and shaking it up. There's far more to sex as a married couple than missionary under the sheets with the lights off for all of five minutes.

Quick tip: The best way to create a desire for sex is to work on improving the intimacy of your marriage without any expectation of sex. Hold your spouse's hand, take them on dates, hug them from behind while they do the washing up. Do all of the little loving things that make them feel special for the sake of doing them, not just to try and get sex out of them. Respark your relationship through nice gestures to demonstrate your love and appreciation, and the sex will follow.

Chapter Six:
Handling Emotional Abuse

While any kind of abuse in any context is horrible and wrong, in this book we'll be focusing mainly on emotional abuse in marriages rather than physical abuse. The latter form tends to be more obvious while emotional abuse is far more subtle and insidious; sometimes neither party is even aware that it is taking place. In this chapter, I'll be coaching you how to handle any emotional abuse that you might face in your marriage.

What is Emotional Abuse?

Emotional abuse is sometimes known as psychological abuse. It is something of an umbrella term used to describe a range of behaviors and patterns of repeated conduct that have a serious negative effect on a person's mental health and sense of well-being. While virtually everyone is aware of what physical abuse is owing to its visibility and obvious and dramatic nature, emotional abuse can often fly low under the radar and fall into a grey area in people's judgment where the bigger picture of abuse that certain isolated, negative, toxic patterns of behavior make up isn't clear.

There a number of different elements that make up emotional abuse. Some of these are:

1. **Intimidation and threats** - This refers to any behavior that is intended to manipulate or pressure you into doing what someone wants. It can be small acts of aggression such as shouting (verbal abuse) or acting aggressively, all the way through to breaking things and threatening to hurt you in some way.

2. **Undermining** - This is the act of eroding your position or making you feel small. It includes things like dismissing your opinion, consistently disagreeing with you, and making you look wrong or stupid in front of others.

3. **Gaslighting** - Gaslighting is when someone tries to make you doubt your own opinion or your recollection of past events. They may prod, poke, outright lie, or try to tell you that you're overreacting, being oversensitive, or remembering something wrong.

4. **Attempts to control you** - A person trying to tell you what you can and can't wear, who you can or can't hang out with, what you eat, what you watch on TV, and what you do with your life all counts as them attempting to control you. Emotionally abusive people seek to order their worlds by keeping the people

in their lives on a short leash and under their control.

5. **Economic abuse** - Withholding money, preventing you from getting a job, or excluding you from having finances of your own all count as economic abuse. It's another form of trying to control you by keeping you dependent on your abuser for financial support.

6. **Being made to feel guilty** - Emotionally abusive people use this as a tactic to motivate others to do what they want by making them feel as though they owe the favor to them somehow or that they would be wrong to refuse.

7. **Excessive criticism** - This is especially relevant when it's part of a pattern of

potshots aimed at taking down your self-esteem or self-value and self-purpose.

It's important to point out that sometimes a person who is perpetrating emotional abuse isn't even aware that what they're doing is even abusive. Some people lack the self-awareness to step back and look at their own behavior in context, and be able to make a rational judgment about what they've been doing and why. Often, emotionally abusive people are simply used to treating the people in their life that way because they've worked out they can make people do what they want through using emotionally abusive techniques. Nobody deserves abuse, but it's all terrifyingly common. It can be perpetrated by anyone and received by anyone, regardless of social role. People emotionally abuse others for all kinds of reasons, most of which have to do with trying to manipulate and control people, as well as making themselves feel better about themselves by putting other people down. This last reason is normally an opportunistic and often thinly veiled sniping at your own value and worth which makes the people who do it feel slightly better about their own self-image, with which they are seriously unhappy. Think of it like someone who's drowning climbing over someone trying to keep them afloat and pushing them underwater in the process of trying to gasp for air.

Emotional abuse can and often does escalate into physical abuse if left unchecked. After becoming sick and tired of being bullied emotionally, some victims who begin to stand up to their abusers can find themselves being attacked or assaulted as a final attempt to dominate and exert control over them. Emotional abuse has a high correlation with domestic violence and physical abuse, so it is vital that anyone suffering from it seeks as much help as possible in order to deal with the problem.

Dealing With Emotional Abuse

Although there are some who may disagree, it has been my experience that the majority of emotionally abusive people aren't actually bad people at heart, although when it comes to physical abuse it becomes harder to make excuses. There are a lot of people out there who never really learn the right way to talk to others or fail to recognize the full consequences of their words beyond their own self interest. Regardless of this, safety should always be the primary concern when trying to handle emotional abuse. It's okay to stand up for yourself, speak up, and get yourself out of the situation you're in. You're entitled to be treated with respect. You deserve better than living under the thumb of somebody else, but be smart, protect yourself, and make sure you get out of that situation. You have to be brave and put yourself first to avoid people taking advantage of you in life.

There are two main approaches towards handling emotional abuse. If the abuse isn't particularly bad, it might be able to be broken by using communication strategies in order to try and reach the other person and show them the effect that their actions and words are having on you. Sitting them down and having a difficult but open and honest conversation about things as you see them might be enough to open someone's eyes as to the true nature of their behavior. Keep in mind that doing this can cause people to become defensive and aggressive, however, so it might be best to do it somewhere relatively public. Another strategy than can be very effective is to first identify emotional abuse, verify it, and then accept it. You can practice this method by picking out when you're on the receiving end of emotional abuse and then flagging it up to your abuser by asking them why they said or did something. Regardless of whether their response is to deflect or be defensive, you can then tell them how what they said or did made you feel and ask them if their intention was to make you feel that way. You then accept whatever their response is and try to reach them by opening their eyes momentarily on the spot right after they've done something negative or toxic. You can then gain an understanding of their motivations and a revelation about their true character and self-awareness. Doing this can help you to curb an abusive person's behavior by more slowly showing them that you understand why they're doing something and that it's hurting you; it can also give you the green light to extract yourself from their lives and make your own way on your own terms. It's a slower approach, but it can be more effective at defusing a person and slowly helping them to change their ways rather than forcing an intervention by having an open and honest discussion about it.

Another method is something known as 'grey rocking'. This technique essentially involves curbing emotionally abusive behavior by withholding the emotional response that they're looking for. This is particularly effective within the context of verbal abuse and criticism, where you have total control over how you respond. If you remain as neutral and as calm and withdrawn from the situation as possible without provoking them, they will eventually begin to get bored with abusing you emotionally as there isn't the satisfying effect of seeing you become upset or snapping back at them. When you don't give an emotionally abusive person the response they're looking for, you're depriving them of their motivation to do it in the first place.

Chapter Seven:
Saving Your Marriage

At this stage in the book, it's time to put everything together and knuckle down in order to address the ultimate question: how do you save your marriage?

Prevent Divorce and Save Your Marriage

Virtually all of us come to a point in our marriage where we have a tough decision to make. Do we give up on things and call it a day, or do we knuckle down and save our marriage? If the former decision is yours, then the next chapter will deal with how to go about putting that into process. I myself am a big advocate of preserving marriages, saving the key relationships in your life, and enriching the bonds you have with people in order to push on together and help each other to a better future. I think we have to work together as a team in order to learn and grow in the right way. Nobody is perfect, and everyone makes mistakes. Every marriage has room for improvement, and you have to work hard in order to be fulfilled and happy with your spouse and they with you. I say stick by them, if you can — but only when both of you being happy and fulfilled together is an option. Never stay with someone if you're only going to be miserable with them.

It's never too late to save your marriage. As I've mentioned previously in this book, I've seen couples who had gone through a whole carnival of carnage throughout the course of their marriage, done each other the world of hurt and had extremely bitter feelings and lots of resentment towards each other come out on the other side of their marriage difficulty as happy, well-adjusted, enlightened and loving people, aware of the true nature of the difficulties of being married and being human and determined to stick together and face life alongside one another rather than going their separate ways. Saving your marriage is an incredibly educational and humbling experience. There's not much quite like it in terms of changing your perspective and the way you think and feel. You become aware of just how much difficulty both you and your spouse are facing in life, and through communication come to understand, accept, and love each other once again.

Saving your marriage is a relatively straightforward — although not easy — process. It's all about making an honest assessment of the direction, velocity, and character of your marriage, and then making a concerted effort alongside your spouse to improve and elevate them. You need to work out what you're doing right as a couple and where you're going wrong, and then try to do more of what works and less of what doesn't. The attitude, mindset and assumptions with which you approach your marriage will determine whether you make it a fulfilling and satisfying part of your life or allow it to be draining and toxic. How you deal with problems makes far more of a difference in your marriage than the nature of the problems themselves.

Everybody is unique, so there are always differences in relationships, no matter how similar to someone else you might feel. Our differences are a good thing — they're essential and interesting, and tell us about who we are as people. However, differences create conflict. How you deal with this conflict is the measure of whether you make or break a marriage. Every relationship experiences conflict from time to time, but how do you treat it? Is it raised voices and regretful comments or calm, understanding, patient dialogue? The choice is yours.

Marriages tend to have a certain tornado-like structure, which is often the result of the chaos we experience in childhood. There is a calm middle ground in the center where we can be together and be level, but as soon as an issue is pushed too far in any one direction the conflict and pain starts. This setup only inevitably leads to hurt and leaves us balancing precariously in the eye of the storm because we're afraid that doing anything to rock the boat might throw everything off kilter and ruin a hard-won peace.

This is the height of neuroticism, but it's part of being human. In general, we lack the understanding and perspective to really be part of a happy and fulfilling life partnership with others. It's only through working hard to change the whole dynamic of your marriage and relationship to one another that you can extract yourselves from this tornado-like system and really begin to appreciate what it means to live life by each other's side.

When you're experiencing difficulty in your marriage, the first thing you have to recognize, accept, and work on is that you're no longer each other's first priority. Somewhere along the line, the marriage has developed in such a way that you've grown further apart than you once were. There's a lack of connection and importance, and you lose each other's hearts. The critical moment when you have this realization as a couple can either be the day the divorce effectively and symbolically happens or the day you decide that you're going to stop this process of losing each other's hearts and work to win them back.

In order to win each other back, you have to think in terms of why you're losing or have lost the connection you had that made you want to get married in the first place or made the two of you fall in love. You have lost somewhere the intimacy in your marriage along the way, and it needs to return. The problem with this is that it can't just be found like a lost object; once it's gone, the only way to get it back is to rebuild it the slow way you did it in the first place. You need to talk to each other in depth about your feelings and the way you experience life. About why you are the way you are and the reasons behind you doing the things you do. You need to go back over the issues that have been molding you from childhood and work out how to move on from the things that have held you back. Part of reconnecting as a couple is bringing the problems you both face out of the subconscious and exposing it to the light. Try to become aware of the reasons why you are the way you are, rather than living your life in misery and ignorance. Just talking about these problems with one another will weaken the hold they have over you, helping you to leave them in the past where they belong.

Sometimes, we don't even remember the influential and traumatic past events that shape us and determine the way we treat ourselves and others. This unconscious programming can often only be uncovered by talking about it. You have to start talking about things for the domino effect to start and things to begin coming back to you and make sense in the wider context of molding you into the person you are today. We have to first examine our own wiring in this way to really begin to change it. Raising your own and your spouse's awareness of the programming you received from childhood, especially from upsetting and traumatic events, is absolutely vital to becoming more well-adjusted people and having a better marriage relationship. Without talking about the things that have happened to you at length or in detail, you're just not able to truly process and deal with them You have to open up in order to let things out and release their control over you. It's the difference between dealing with the source and root of the problem or merely treating the symptoms. When you learn to overcome your subconscious programming, it becomes easier to look at things objectively and tackle them together, rather than just blaming each other for your problems.

The deeper the conversation gets in any relationship, the closer the people in it become. The more you talk about your problems with your spouse, the more the two of you will reconnect. As the two of you talk, you should make a mutual commitment to changing the nature of your marriage. It's very important that you're both on the same page about this. You need to both want to make your marriage a happy, balanced, fulfilling thing to be a part of. For that, you both need to understand how to go about doing this and be prepared to put in the work to make it so. Learning to look at things positively is of paramount importance, as is understanding that nothing is ever perfect and that there is always more to be done. Like anything in life, having a great marriage is a matter of choice. Although it's only once you see that it's a choice that it becomes one. Your attitude towards and position on your marriage influence where you look and how you compare your own married relationship to that of other married couples. This is also known as selection bias. If you feel like your marriage is awful, you will be far more likely to take note of and compare your marriage to another one when the other seems better than yours. In the same way, feeling good about your marriage makes you more likely to compare it to poorer marriages. In truth, every marriage is good and bad. It is what it is. It could always be better, it could always be worse — and that's the way things will always be.

It's essential that you begin the healing process as soon as you can — ideally before you fall out of love completely, although it is almost always possible to claw back to it with enough hard work; the problem with falling out of love is that it removes the motivation to work hard on your marriage in the first place, as it no longer seems to be worth it. Whatever stage you and your spouse are at, keep in mind that these things take time. There's no quick or easy fix when it comes to relationships. You have to just consistently put the work in and see how things pan out in the long run. Divorce is a permanent solution to a temporary problem, so try to keep in mind the bigger picture that you're aiming for and remember to try and see all of the positivity and beauty that exists in your marriage *right now*, and all the good things that you and your spouse could do and create in the near future once you're back on track. This attitude and proactivity in demonstrating how much your spouse means to you is what will keep your marriage alive, even if it's on life support.

There's a stark contrast between doing what is easy and doing what is right. Doing the right thing as one half of a married couple is rarely ever easy, but that doesn't mean that you have an excuse not to do it. Being married is a difficult enterprise, but it's richly rewarding as long as you're willing to do what the work to make it that way. Marriage has to be intimate and highly involved to work; otherwise, you won't enjoy touching, talking, or being around each other.

Only the right attitude, principles, values, and outlooks can generate this intimacy being shared and expressed by both you and your spouse. Try to bring inspiration and energy to your marriage. Be creative. Seek to build things together, not destroy them. Use your thoughts, use your language, and use your trust to steer the two of you in the right direction.

Saving Your Marriage Alone

Marriage is a team sport. If you're not working together in at least some capacity or there's some willingness from both sides to save the marriage, it's not going to work. That being said, there are times when one person is far more invested in saving a marriage than their spouse is, and is placed in the impossible position of having to try to make it work all by themselves. Although it does take two to tango, there are often valid reasons why one spouse is willing to put in much more effort than their partner that aren't because they're totally uninterested and want things to end. People are incredibly complicated and impossibly complex. Picking apart how you feel and why you feel that way is a difficult thing to do, and sometimes we just get lost in limbo where nothing seems to mean anything. That doesn't mean that we'll feel that way forever.

If you feel like your spouse isn't doing as much or isn't as interested in saving your marriage as you are, you're put in a challenging situation. Obviously, it's one that can't last forever. You can't carry your marriage single-handedly for the rest of your lives, nor should you want to. Maneuvering out of this place involves getting your partner back on board and engaged by acting unilaterally and making sure that you are doing all that you can do to make things better between you. If even after you've demonstrated what your marriage means to you and how hard you're willing to fight for it your spouse still shows little interest in putting in more effort to make things better, it might be a lost cause. In the meantime, all you can do is try.

The first thing to accept when it comes to saving your marriage on your own is that your spouse is already putting in all they're going to put in for the time being. There's no quick fix or easy way to get them engaged and fighting for your marriage. No, it's not fair, and yes, they should do more, but in all probability, if they haven't done so already then they will not start any time soon. There is nothing you can do to change or control them or make them take things seriously. Any attempts to do so will likely only make things between the two of you worse. Instead, you'll have to focus on knuckling down, getting into the trenches, and doing the heavy lifting yourself, for now. You're getting all you can out of your spouse currently, so it will have to be enough until they come around and start pulling their weight.

The process of saving your marriage single-handedly doesn't deviate too much from the rest of the advice I've already laid out throughout this book. The difference is that you have to be far more committed and driven in order to do these things by yourself without your partner doing the same thing. You will become fed up and disillusioned. You will wonder why you ever even try. But if you persist and hang in there, your positivity, love, kindness, and effort will begin to rub off on your partner. After all, the best way to get the two of you out of the quicksand is sometimes to work to free yourself first and then come back to help. The attitudes and behavior of the people around us rub off on us, so if you can put the ideas we've discussed in this book to work single-handedly, you will more likely than not be able to bring your partner around to seeing things from a healthier, more positive point of view.

Gratitude and positivity give you the power and the perspective you need to be able to push on and tackle everything else. They will also help to cultivate the same characteristics in your partner. As human beings, we're naturally hard-wired to evaluate everything in our lives. This means that we tend to judge things simply as a force of habit. However, this judgment is a choice and something that we can reconsider to develop an attitude of openness and interest without jumping to negative conclusions straight away. A lot of marriages feature something known as 'blame outsourcing', where we judge and place the blame for our problems on our partners when really we have at least a contributory role to all of the issues in our life. This might be the case for you or your spouse; it's likely that there's an element of this in both of your attitudes towards each other. Understanding this can help us to take responsibility for our problems and focus on doing what we can and should to do hold up our end of the deal, keep our vows, and do everything we can to save our marriage, even if that means acting alone at first.

The Pressure of Having Children

One of the most central elements of most marriages and a common cause of stress, pressure, and conflict is having children. Even before a child is conceived, the very concept of one can put a serious strain on any relationship. Having a baby is a significant economic, time, and social investment, and for this reason issues of practicality and timing inevitably surface. Even within the context of a marriage, the topic of having children can be a difficult subject. It's for this reason that it's so important that both you and your spouse are as clear as you can be about your own and each other's expectations when it comes to having children to avoid disappointment if they significantly differ.

Having children changes a relationship in a number of deep and fundamental ways. If you have kids, then it's important that you compensate for the effect they inevitably have on your marriage in order to keep it healthy and happy. They bring a vast amount of pressure and stress into the relationship dynamic between their caregivers, who have to make sure they provide their children with food, clothes, quality time, love, and the stimulation that they need to grow and develop in a healthy manner. The combined effect of all of this can put a lot of strain on even the strongest marriage.

Every relationship needs maintenance, especially during times of change. Having a child is possibly the most extraordinary and boundary-pushing experience a person can have, so it's even more important that you give your marriage the time and effort it deserves, rather than neglecting it to focus your attention on your children. It's incredibly easy to become absorbed by our children; after all, we're genetically coded to put them before ourselves in every way. You have to maintain the other relationships in your life, though, and very few of these are more important than the one you have with your spouse. Make sure you're taking time for your marriage and attempting to spend time alone with your spouse. This might mean having someone else watch the kids while the two of you go out for a date night together, or simply making the effort to cuddle, kiss, and watch a movie together after the kids have gone to sleep. You need to spend time together as a couple to remember that you're not just parents; you're married. You're lovers, best friends, and better halves first and foremost, although it can be easy to lose sight of this. Make sure you take the time to rekindle things from time to time and allow yourselves to be comfortable just being alone and spending time together to maintain the strength of your marriage and the bond you have with each other.

Another important thing to do to keep your marriage strong when you have children is to remember to take care of yourself. If your own immediate needs aren't met, how can you expect to be a good husband, wife, or parent? The single most important relationship we have in life is the one we have with ourselves. If you're not doing the things you need to do to look after yourself, then your marriage will inevitably suffer, along with every other aspect of your life. It can be very hard to remember to take the time to be alone and do the things that you enjoy doing, the things that revive and refresh you and leave you feeling revitalized. A common side effect of having children is feeling less individual, less like an autonomous human being, and more like the social role you have to play for your family. Everyone needs their alone time, time spent doing what they love and seeing their friends. Without this, the relationships in our lives inevitably suffer. If you want to save your marriage, then make sure both you and your spouse are taking time for yourselves.

Quick tip: You're not in this alone. Everybody needs a support network, people around them to enjoy life with when things are good and to help share the burden when times get rough. Your spouse and children represent a great support network for you, but make sure that you don't neglect yourself or your friends while enjoying family life. Through you and your spouse remembering to spend time on each other and yourselves, you will help to cultivate a peaceful, caring, loving home environment for everyone in your family.

Bonus: Date Night Ideas for Married Couples

When it comes to spending quality time with your spouse, you're not just taking time to enjoy yourselves. You're reconnecting as a couple. You're strengthening the bond and the intimacy that the two of you share, and these will be the factors that enable you to go the distance together. Besides, you only live your life once.

You have to have fun and enjoy yourself, and who better to share recreational activities with than the person you married because you wanted to spend the rest of your life with them?

I'd recommend making at least one allocated night of the week date night, such as Friday or Saturday, and sticking to it every week as far as you possibly can. This gives the two of you something to look forward to at the end of the week and ensures that you're consistently spending quality time together. You can also talk about and plan what you're going to do every weekend throughout the course of the week, which builds tension and excitement and ensures you're always coming up with fun ideas.

While part of the fun of having a weekly date night is planning what to do with your spouse or being spontaneous, I've included a few ideas to help get you started:

1. **Dinner and a movie** - This is a classic, but it's a classic for good reason. Going out for a romantic dinner with your spouse before heading to see a movie at the cinema makes for a fun, intimate date night. It's a good mix of conversation and passive entertainment where you can sit back, relax, and enjoy a show together while holding hands. You can even extend it afterwards before going home by going for a walk or a drive somewhere together. All in all, I always vouch for this as one of the top date ideas of all time. It's versatile, effective, and thoroughly enjoyable, plus you get to eat a nice meal and then have popcorn and a soda.

2. **Going for drinks** - This is another classic. There's nothing quite like kicking back at the bar or in the privacy of a booth and getting a bit too drunk with your spouse. After all, dates are about having fun, and drinking

certainly facilitates that! You can have hours and hours of conversation, flirting, and building intimacy with nothing but the two of you and a handful of drinks each. Alcohol can really help to break the ice, too, especially if the two of you have been going through a rough patch and aren't sure how to go about rebuilding the intimacy. Going for drinks can also take you back to when you were dating, and all of the excitement and anticipation that comes along with it. Just make sure you have a ride home!

3. **Bowling** - Playing games together is a lot of fun. You can laugh, joke, and innocently poke fun at each other in a way that really builds the camaraderie and intimacy between the two of you. Being married is about being great friends, and fun activities like bowling are an excellent way to maintain your friendship or spice things up and

remind yourselves of who you are to each other when you've been feeling distant.

4. **Going to the beach** - This is an often overlooked but extremely rewarding date experience in my opinion — provided you're near a beach. You can go during the day when it's warm and swim and sunbathe or read or listen to music while eating ice cream together, or at night with some blankets and look at the stars while listening to the waves rolling in. This kind of date is especially magical if it's not the kind of thing you'd normally do together, just the two of you. It evokes the feeling of being young and in love all over again, something that I know many marriages are sorely lacking.

5. **Dessert** - Going for dessert together is a great, if short, date idea, particularly fulfilling if it's spur of the moment or you've

already been doing something together. It's a great way to top off the evening and spend some time reflecting on what you've done previously, although it's a solid standalone date idea in itself; especially if the place you get dessert packs a serious punch.

6. **Theatre** - Much like going to the movies, going to the theatre with your spouse is a recipe for a brilliant date. You also have the added bonus of an interlude and the novelty of seeing actors performing live, something that can be an incredibly powerful and moving experience. If you have the opportunity to go and see one of the big Broadway-esque musicals you should jump at it; they're mind blowingly good fun and will have the two of you talking about it together for days afterwards. Dates like this allow you to do something before and/or after too, meaning you can tailor the

experience to get as much out of it as you desire.

7. **Outdoor activities** - These may not be everyone's idea for a great date, but for some people they're magical. You should try to allocate whole days to things like this rather than evenings. There's something about being out in the wilderness hiking on a trail with your spouse, or riding bikes, or taking a boat out on a lake together that inspires overwhelming feelings of love, gratitude, and appreciation. Spending time together in the great outdoors is a humbling and intimate experience, if you're that way inclined. It doesn't have to be anything dramatic or intense, either. You could go for a picnic together, or even a walk. Fresh air and the company of your spouse are all you really need for a great date, sometimes.

8. **Going on vacation** - Whether you finally decide to take that trip to Europe or you're not traveling that far, taking a trip somewhere with your spouse is a very personal and thoroughly fulfilling thing to do. It places the emphasis for both of you on hanging out and spending leisure time together for days at a time, giving you a break from ordinary working life and providing you with a chance to relax together and get to know one another all over again.

9. **Game nights** - A lot of people shrink from the idea of game nights as a way to have fun, but I've always found them to be brilliant. Whether you get a good two-player game or you meet up with other couples and friends for a group activity, playing games is an excellent way to build intimacy and bond with your spouse.

10. **Quiet nights in** - Sometimes, all you need to have fun is the pleasure of each other's company and a night at home together. I find that the simplest dates are often the most rewarding, and spending quality time together can be as simple or as complicated as you want to make it. Nights in can be especially rewarding when one of you cooks for the other, or you cook a meal together and share a bottle of wine, some dessert, and a movie. Being in the comfort of your own home can really add to the atmosphere, too.

Chapter Eight:
Divorce

You probably wouldn't be reading or listening to this book if you were certain you wanted a divorce, but I want this to be a totally inclusive guide, and a handbook for saving marriage wouldn't be complete without a caveat about how to go about ending it the right way. It's a shame, but all things must come to an end one way or another, and sometimes people just aren't meant to be together. If your mind lingers on thoughts about separating from your spouse or they seem to have it in mind themselves, then this chapter is for you.

When Should You Get Divorced?

The question of when it's right to stay and fight for your marriage and when it's best to cut your losses and call it a day is a difficult one to answer. As I've previously mentioned, I am a big advocate of married couples remaining together if they possibly can, if they can find a way to make things work between them and be happy and fulfilled together, and I maintain that most couples can — far more than actually do so. Throwing in the towel is the easy way out, and as the sky-high divorce rates for remarried people goes to show, staying married is far more a process of tenacity and persistence than it is about marrying the right person in the first place. Willpower is everything, and with enough drive and a little guidance virtually any couple can learn how to make their marriage work. Sometimes, however, this just isn't the case. Life tends unfold in the strangest of ways, and many, if not most married people at some point find thoughts of getting divorced coming to them all too readily.

You're not wrong for considering divorce, nor would you be wrong to go through with the process. At the end of the day, the most important thing in your life is you own happiness and well-being, and you have to do whatever you need to protect that. You know the details of your marriage better than anyone, along with your spouse. If you're convinced that there's nothing there worth saving, or you don't want to save it, then you should honor those feelings. Life is too short to be unhappy. You'll know if divorce is the right call or if there's still something between you and your spouse that's worth fighting for. Sometimes people just don't end up working well together; when happiness together becomes an unattainable pipe dream, regardless of the attitude and mindset and willingness to try and improve things from each half of the couple, then it's probably game over, unless you'd prefer to spend the rest of your life in misery.

Deciding whether or not you should get divorced is never something that should be taken lightly. I'd recommend trying to get all the space and perspective you can when you're trying to make up your mind. If you can get out of the house for a few days, or find some other way to have less contact with your spouse other than for essential purposes for a short while, you may find it helps to shift the way you see things and more thoroughly understand what it is that you want from your life, and whether or not your spouse can be a part of that. Talking things through with close friends and family is also a great idea as it can help you to work out how you truly think and feel about your marriage and whether you want to hang in there and try to make things work or you're ready to move on. If you believe that the time is right to draw a line under everything and get a divorce, then that is what you should do. You have to trust yourself and your own judgment; you have to believe in yourself and have your own back. If you won't stand up for yourself and your own happiness and well-being and do what's right for you, then who will?

What to do When Your Spouse Wants to Divorce

If you're in a situation where your spouse has told you that they want to get a divorce, the first thing that you need to do is take a deep breath and try to stay calm. It isn't the end of the world. Keep breathing, stay out of crisis mode. If you start to panic, you'll slip into fight-or-flight mode which will impede your ability to think calmly and clearly. Now, the next few steps you take depends entirely on the full context of your situation; your marriage, the way your spouse feels about your marriage, and the way you feel about it. Perhaps you will end up getting divorced, but maybe you won't. Just because your spouse is saying they want one doesn't necessarily mean that it will end up being what the two of you decide to do. Nothing is set in stone. If you do end up getting divorced, it will be because that course of action is the best for both of you. Whatever happens, your future will be full of happiness and laughter and joy because you possess the power to make it so.

What needs to happen next is important but not urgent, so take the time to process things and get your mind straight before you jump into the next phase. Firstly, you need to try and make an accurate assessment of the reality of your marriage situation. Does your spouse really want a divorce? How do you know? Do you want to get divorced? How do you know? Talk to your spouse about it as openly, honestly, calmly, and maturely as the two of you can possibly manage, and get everything out in the open. This is make or break, so lay all of the cards you're holding out on the table and encourage your spouse to do the same. Focus on what is wrong, not who is wrong. There's obviously something that's not working, or you wouldn't be in this situation, so it's time to get to the bottom of what is broken and why. Tell your spouse exactly how you feel and what you'd like to do in order to proceed, and ask them to do the same. It may be that your spouse really *wants* to make things work, but is at the end of their tether and feels like perhaps divorce might be the only option. How this interaction goes and the conclusions that you come to as a couple will be determined by your individual situation and the context of your marriage. It might be that the two of you agree to give one another another chance to change things, to take one last shot at really making your marriage work.

If, for whatever reason — be it their decision or a mutual one — the two of you are headed for divorce, then the most important thing that you can do is to accept the reality of the situation. If there's nothing more to be done and one or both minds have been made up, then it is what it is. You simply have to accept that things don't always work out the way you might have once thought they would, and that that's okay. It's sad, but it's necessary. If there was another way out, the two of you would have taken it, but this is the end of the line for your marriage. Give yourself as much time and space as you need in order to process this. It might feel like your life is over and the world is ending, but I sincerely promise you that it's not. This might be the end of the current chapter, but it's far from the end of your story; it's the beginning of a whole new chapter.

It doesn't matter how old you are, or how afraid you are that you'll never find love again. You can and will find whatever it is that you want to find from the future. No one deserves to be unhappy, so take comfort in the fact that at least that is coming to an end. You wouldn't be in the position you're in if it wasn't for a whole lot of unhappiness, whether that was on your part or your spouse's.

Sometimes, things just don't work out, and marriage is no exception to this. The very best thing you can do is frame the divorce in your mind as one big learning experience. While it's far from a desirable thing to be going through, it will teach you important lessons about yourself, others, and life that you can take forward with you to become a more well-rounded and experienced person. The difficulties we face in life serve to reveal to us exactly who we are and teach us fundamental lessons about what it means to be human. If you can see the beauty in that, you can take all of the positives (and there will be positives, no matter how hard that may be to believe) from your divorce forwards with you while learning all you can from the negatives and then letting them go to move on with your life in a whole new direction.

Don't fall into the trap of thinking that your main priority should be to find someone else, fast. Getting divorced, like all things in life, is an opportunity. It's a chance to figure out more about who you are and embrace all the things you want to do in life that you might not have been as easily able to do when you were married. Personal development is the inevitable result of any relationship coming to an end, and should strive to embrace this wholeheartedly. There are many, many people stuck in miserable marriages that they can't escape from, and no matter the context of your own marriage, you at least have the freedom to live life on your own terms and make the most out of the time you have to appreciate the incredible experience we call life.

Divorcing Peacefully

Once it's clear that divorce is inevitable, the only thing that's left to do is try to get through the whole process as civilly and amicably as you possibly can. Once the path of divorce has been chosen by one of you, both of you are on it, regardless of whether or not you want to be. If it was your choice to split up, then own it; if this is truly what you want, then don't cave. If it wasn't your choice, all you can do is accept the path you're on and try to make things as easy for both of you as possible. Divorces can get messy fast, especially when it comes to things like finances and custody of children if you have any. Just because your marriage is ending doesn't mean the process has to be full of resentment, bitterness, and hostility. Try to look at it as the final problem that you'll have to work together as a team on. It's possible to do it sensibly and maturely and compassionately as long as you exercise self control and don't do anything intentionally malicious. Just because things are coming to an end doesn't mean spite or nastiness has to be a part of it. All you can do is control your own reactions and conduct, so make sure you're always the bigger person if your soon to be ex seems intent on not playing fair.

Do your best to make the divorce a blameless process, if at all possible. You can only do you part in this, of course, but by avoiding placing blame on your spouse you won't be antagonizing them or provoking a legal shoving match. Focus on the bigger picture; your future once this is all said and done, when the process of getting divorced is just a distant memory far over the horizon in the rear-view mirror. Ugly divorces are very rarely planned. They're most often the result of the situation becoming a quagmire of bad feelings and game-playing, where retaliation for real or perceived unfairness provokes a tit for tat dynamic that quickly spirals out of control and ruins any chance for things to proceed amicably. You always have a choice as to how you act and react. If you act in good faith, with dignity and respect for yourself and your spouse, then the chances are good that your spouse will return the gesture and any ugliness can be averted. Getting divorced is a difficult enough process in the first place; there's no reason to make it any harder than it needs to be.

Some of the best advice I can give to anyone going through a divorce is to get a lawyer, delete Facebook, and hit the gym. There are a number of reasons why this combination is so effective at helping the process along and making everything much easier to deal with. For one, your lawyer will deal with any and all legal formalities, providing you with a degree of separation and invaluable expertise that helps you to avoid the messier and more complicated parts of a divorce, especially if you're trying to make it a peaceful separation but your ex-spouse isn't on board with this. Getting off of social media will help you to clear your head. Going through a divorce comes with a lot of social fallout, and steering clear of social media allows you to avoid getting hung up on anything and instead just focus on your own life. After the dust settles, anyone you still want to keep in your life will still be a part of it, social media or not, and everyone else will be in the past where they belong.

As I previously mentioned, perhaps the stickiest area when it comes to divorce is the matter of children, if you have any with your ex. Who gets custody, what the visitation rights are, and things like child support can become a minefield. Having a lawyer will help you out massively with such complicated legal procedures, but in order to make the process of divorce as easy and as peaceful as possible I'd recommend thinking very deeply about the broader context of the situation and what the fairest thing is for your children. You should always try to put them first, in any situation, even if what is best for them isn't what's best for you. Trying to remain friends, or at least on somewhat positive terms with your ex-spouse is also important if you have children, because to some extent you will continue to be involved in each other's lives for matters of cooperative parenting. This isn't possible in every case, obviously, but you should strive for it as far as you can in order to make things easier in the long run.

Moving On

Learning how to move on after going through a divorce can be a very confusing and even overwhelming process. There will be many things that you have to come to grips with, lots of different areas of your life that you must think about for the first time in a long time. You'll feel a whole range of emotions, from being happy and relieved that your marriage is over, particularly if you were unhappy for a long time, to desperately sad, anxious, confused, and alone. Throughout this process, it's crucial that you focus on yourself as an individual, and do the things that you need to do to encourage your own personal development and set yourself up for a better future. Moving on from divorce is a process of recovery. It's about learning how to be on your own again. It's a tough process, but you'll get through it with time, and emerge on the other side a better, wiser person for having had the experience.

An important step towards recovery is understanding what went wrong. Why you married in the first place, and why you ended up getting divorced. Everyone makes mistakes; what's important is that you learn from them. Lots of people get caught up in this process, lingering on questions like 'what did I do wrong?' 'Whose fault is all this?' and 'Why is this happening to me?' But I think the only way to really move on is to realize that it's no one's fault, that no one is to blame, and that life is simply one big learning experience. It's only once you can put the feeling of having to have something to blame and hate for your negative experiences to bed that you can finally begin to see life for what it truly is. It just is. There doesn't have to be a rhyme or reason. It can be helpful to instead focus on what the relationship was lacking and the ways that you and your ex were incompatible just because of who you are. There are problems in every relationship, and they ended up being too much for yours. That's okay. No one is to blame. Your marriage was lacking something and failed to meet you or your spouse's needs in some way. It's better to contemplate questions along this line and look at the whole thing objectively, rather than focusing on who did what and whose fault everything is. Looking at things this way might be more upsetting, but it will help you to gain a clearer understanding of the truth of the situation. The greater your understanding, the easier it will be for you to move on.

The period just after separation and divorce is a chance to reflect, to take an inventory of your life so far and find out where your trajectory is headed, and think about how to change it if you so desire. It's a chance to get your head straight, to find your individuality and work out what kind of person you really want to be, on no one else's terms except your own. Looking after yourself and committing to good habits is vital at this stage, as the first few months are when the reality of the situation really sets in and the time that you will feel most lost and directionless. Your self-esteem and self-confidence may take a hard knock during this time, so it's essential that you do the following things in order to get back up from being knocked down:

1. **Grieve**: A divorce is a massively traumatic life event. So much changes and you're left feeling very different to how you might have been not that long ago. Give yourself the time you need to grieve for the part of your life that has ended, regardless of whether or not you wanted it to. It takes time for reality to settle in and for you to get used to the way things will be from now on. You'll have good days and bad days, so support yourself by allowing yourself to feel the negative emotions you're experiencing.

2. **Let go:** In order to truly move on with your life, you have to come to terms with everything that has happened and allow yourself to let go. The pain and anger you feel can make you feel powerful and strong; they're almost addictive in this sense. Feel how you feel, and honor how you feel, but then when it's time, let go. The more strongly

you hold onto your negative emotions, the harder it will be to sever the connection you have to your past and really move on.

3. **Talk to people:** Not only will talking to people help you to process your thoughts and feelings, but it will also prevent isolation and help you to maintain a healthy sense of perspective. You're not alone. Sharing your inner world with the people you're close with will enable you to better cope with the situation you're in.

4. **Set yourself goals:** Some days it might feel like you're going nowhere fast, and that's okay. I find it can be helpful to plan ahead and set yourself some short term goals in order to give yourself a schedule to stick to and things to keep you occupied. Make sure any targets you set yourself are achievable,

and don't hold it against yourself if you fail to meet all of them.

5. **Look after yourself:** Make sure that you're getting enough sleep each night, eating healthily, and getting enough exercise. If you're not taking good care of yourself, you'll begin to feel more depressed, lethargic, and negative about your life.

6. **Seek help:** If you need help, never be ashamed to ask for it. Friends, therapists, counselors — there are plenty of options for you to speak to people and get real help when you're struggling. You don't have to suffer alone.

One of the things people struggle particularly hard with in the divorce's wake is a sense of loss and failure. This feeling can strike particularly hard if you've experienced some kind of reduction in your standard of living or quality of life after your divorce, such as having to move to a smaller house or apartment or even staying on somebody's couch. At such moments, the world can seem to shrink around you, and the feeling of loss of the sense of safety and security that you once had and now don't can threaten to overwhelm you. This feeling can also strike when you realize that the family dynamic has changed when you're with your kids and your ex-spouse isn't there or you wake up to an empty house without them. It's helpful to remember at times like this that things will get better and you won't always feel this way. We tend to look back on the past with rose-tinted glasses, especially when it's something we miss. Your situation isn't the worst thing that could happen to you, and it's far better than being trapped in an unhappy marriage.

Quick tip: With time, your situation and outlook *will* improve. You'll have a better place from which to get your perspective and feel more familiar with your new lease of life. You'll find love again, in time, and with the lessons you've learned, you'll be able to avoid repeating the mistakes of the past. Being optimistic for the future can be hard, but if you can focus on reclaiming your individuality and living your life the way you want to live then you will feel better about things.

Final Words

Being married and getting divorced are things that more and more of us are going through as we move slowly into the 21st century. I think that now, more than ever, it's essential that we have a clear idea of the difficulties involved in maintaining a lifelong commitment to another person, and just how hard it can be to make things work. Too many people enter into marriage with the idea that things are going to be relatively easy, because they have a mindset of 'it's us' or the idea that they will somehow be exempt from something that married people almost unanimously agree is extremely hard work. I wrote this book because I like to help people. It's the reason I've been practicing as a therapist for so long. I wanted to condense my thoughts and experiences of coaching people through how to stay together and how to begin to address life once more after splitting up.

It's my belief that virtually every marriage can be saved, as long as both partners are willing to try. At their core, all these things really require are dedication and hard work. I make a strong exception for abusive or otherwise extremely unhappy marriages — there are circumstances under which making things work is either an impossible or unattractive prospect — but for most people, in regular, run-of-the-mill marriages with their fair share of ups and downs, making their marriage work is simply a matter of attitude and mindset. From my professional experience, I've learned that there truly is no mountain too high to climb, no obstacle too difficult to overcome. I've seen couples go through hell, go through the worst drama and most horrible experiences that you can imagine, and emerge on the other side stronger for having been through the ordeal. No matter what has happened in the past, there is nothing that can't be put right in the present if both partners are on the same page about wanting to do this.

Teamwork is everything in relationships, and this is especially true in marriage. The lawful act of union represents the pinnacle of intimacy and closeness. As human beings, each of us has an entire world, a whole universe of feelings and thoughts inside of us. Sharing that in such an incredibly intimate and vulnerable way is an extremely difficult thing to do, especially when it means having the difficult conversations that we might not want to have. Who can say why we go through the multitude of difficult circumstances that we do? Things seem to happen to us almost by accident, with us not realizing the true significance of the things we're doing until we're knee-deep in a situation we never imagined we could become stuck in before.

This is why it's so important to be kind and compassionate in our marriages and elsewhere in life. Life unfolds in the strangest of ways, and if we can't be totally open and honest with the person we've pledged our life to, then who? Who can we turn to in our darkest moments when we've made terrible mistakes and desperately in need of forgiveness? It isn't easy, but nothing ever is. We have to be able to keep the bigger picture in mind and forgive each other for our wrongs. We have to be able to sit down and work out how we're going to get through this, rather than pointing fingers and playing the blame game every time someone slips up.

We have to be honest to ourselves and our spouses, no matter how hard that might be. We have to be capable of rebuilding trust when it's broken. We have to be able to understand and forgive when all we want to do is scream and judge and hate. If we refuse to turn the other cheek, if we're incapable of humbling ourselves and realizing that it could all too easily be us begging forgiveness and crying with regret and despair, then we can't expect to participate in the endeavor of life as a married person.

The hurdles that are presented to us throughout the course of married life are numerous and difficult to vault, but it is always possible. Whether you're dealing with infidelity, porn addiction, a dead bedroom, or emotional abuse, it is your outlook on yourself, on your life, on your spouse, and on the marriage you share together that will determine whether you're capable of working through it and moving on together with a better understanding of each other or check out as soon as things get hard. While no one can ever tell you when you should stay to try to make things work or when you should leave it all behind, I can tell you that no matter who you are married to, things will never be perfect. Making mistakes is a part of being human, and every marriage experiences its fair share of misgivings, missteps, and regret.

It is my sincere hope that with this book, everyone reading or listening to it may be able to better understand themselves and the circumstances and difficulties of their marriage.

I've shown you what it takes to save your marriage by walking you through advice applicable both in general and in a set of specific circumstances; the rest is up to you to put into practice. I've tried to instill in you the knowledge that all these things boil down to is your willingness and ability to adapt and persevere. The rest is irrelevant.

Remember that marriage, for all of its difficulties and ordeals, is beautiful. Being successfully married is largely about being able to step back and look at the bigger picture to appreciate the wider context of the journey you're on together and just how lucky you are to have someone beside you who you can call your lover, best friend, and life partner, someone whom you can show forgiveness to and receive it in return, someone who you can love and hold in their worst moments and their best. Marriage is hard work, like anything that's worth doing in life. The trick is to go into it knowing it's going to be painful, knowing that it will hurt at times, but understanding that it will also be beautiful, full of light and love and laughter. Everybody hurts you sooner or later, and you hurt everybody in the exact same way. The trick is to find someone who you're willing to hurt for.

www.ingramcontent.com/pod-product-compliance
Lightning Source LLC
Chambersburg PA
CBHW020239130626
46549CB00005B/1974